THIS BOOK BELONGS TO

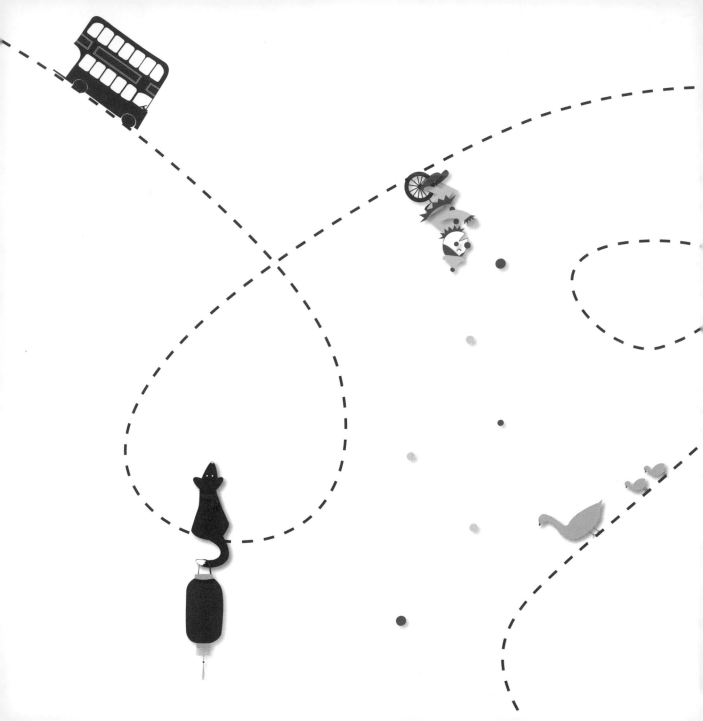

LITTLE LONDON

CHILD-FRIENDLY DAYS OUT AND FUN THINGS TO DO

by Kate Hodges and Sunshine Jackson

Virgin BOOKS

To my amazing daughters, whose energy,
imagination and sense of wonder were the
inspiration behind Hopscotch and *Little London*,
and to my brilliantly unconventional parents
who continue to pass on their spirit of
adventure to their grandchildren.
SUNSHINE

To Gareth, Arthur and Dusty, Gloria and Jeannie
for being inspirational and entertaining co-pilots
around this wonderful city.
KATE

CONTENTS

INTRODUCTION

Little London is the book we've been wishing we had on our shelves since we had our children: a truly useful guide to spending time in London with kids. Arranged month by month, it is packed with affordable, imaginative, exciting and fun things to do at every time of year, and brimming with hidden gems and handy hints for getting the best out of your London adventures.

Little London started life in 2010 as a weekly email for parents called the Hopscotch Newsletter. Having been enthusiastic, adventurous Londoners before having our children, we were nevertheless struggling to find interesting stuff to do around town now that we had kids in tow. Online searches turned up expensive theatre trips or uncurated listings sites with no hints about what was really worth a visit, or where to find a child-friendly café when hunger meltdowns threatened. Individual museum and venue websites were too big and too numerous to trawl through with small children on our hands. And we simply couldn't find any of the quirky, magical and off-the-beaten track events and locations that we knew to be all over our favourite city.

Soon realising that all our best outings had been recommended by other parents, we resolved to create a weekly newsletter by parents for parents. In the newsletter and the book we aim to suggest as broad a spread of activities as possible. From our own parenting experience, we know that some of our kids are wild about playing pirates and running around wide-open spaces, while others enjoy focused art activities. And everyone benefits from insider knowledge – how to avoid the queues, or how to make the journey there and back an adventure too. In short, we aim to distil the experience of as many parents as we can find for the benefit of all parents, grandparents, godparents, nannies, aunts, uncles (we could go on!) and the children they accompany around London. We hope we've put together an inspiring guide for adults and children that will be thumbed through time and time again.

The book is broken down into months, with loads of seasonal suggestions, and at the end of each entry there's all the information you'll need for your visit: opening times, websites, phone numbers, addresses and nearest tubes or other transport. You'll also find suggestions for stuff to look out for or to avoid, and extra nuggets of local knowledge.

On 25 of the entries you will spot a ★. This means that the event, activity or attraction is one of our very favourite ways to spend a day out – totally unmissable!

In addition to all the out-and-about-in-London inspiration, you'll find some great recipes and craft activities, because sometimes a quiet day at home feels like the best plan.

We hope you love reading this book as much as we've loved making it. If we have included something, it is because we really believe it to be worth a visit. London is a fantastic city for children, full of free and good-value activities and events, with the traditional and the very modern nestling side by side from north to south, east to west. There really is something for everyone. Make a plan; get out and about; have an adventure!

Sunshine and Kate x

Sign up for free weekly updates to accompany this book at thehopscotchnewsletter.com

Key to symbols

FREE	no one has to pay
£	adult tickets are £0–£5
££	adult tickets are £5–£10
£££	adult tickets are £10+
♘	accessible by buggy
♿	accessible by wheelchair
☕	on-site café
🚇	the nearest tube, DLR or Overground stations, all within a 10-minute walk

This book's pricing guide is based on adult ticket prices. If kids go free to a venue, we'll make that clear. All information is correct at time of press, but you should always check the venue or event's website ahead of time to make sure you're up to date.

Useful websites

- Sign up to the Hopscotch Newsletter: thehopscotchnewsletter.com
- Plan your journey: journeyplanner.tfl.gov.uk
- Get two-for-one tickets to big attractions: daysoutguide.co.uk

Have we missed somewhere or something? Let us know at info@thehopscotchnewsletter.com

CELEBRATE
NEW YEAR'S DAY,
AMERICAN STYLE*

Very little early risers don't give you a post-party lie-in, so you'll probably be up first thing on New Year's Day. Make the most of your alarm call and get yourselves, bright-eyed and bushy-tailed, down to the spectacular New Year's Day Parade.

More than 10,000 performers, including bands, cheerleaders, dancers, huge floats and even the *actual* Queen's horses of 'Humpty Dumpty' fame throng the streets of central London for this free, fun carnival. It kicks off at 11.45am on Piccadilly outside the Ritz Hotel, travels through Piccadilly Circus and Trafalgar Square, down Whitehall and ends in Parliament Street.

We like to watch the parade from Trafalgar Square; it has a big screen relaying all the action, so if your kids are really small and can't get to the front of the crowd, they can still see what's going on. You need to get there pretty early to get a good viewing point, so take a hot drink and something to stave off boredom. Go easy the night before and enjoy.

londonparade.co.uk
FREE &
Parade runs 11.45am–3pm
Westminster, Charing Cross, Piccadilly Circus
Don't forget to pick up your free copy of commemorative newspaper The Parade Post *– it's a great souvenir for kids.*

ESCAPE WINTER IN THE BALMY BARBICAN CONSERVATORY

Shhhhhh! Don't tell a soul, but there's a secret, warm place where parents can hang out and chill and kids can wander in wonder. It's slap-bang in the middle of the city, full of exotic plants, birds and fish – and it's under cover and cosy.

The second-biggest conservatory in London is tucked away at the Barbican, and is open to visitors most Sundays (check the website for more details). It's a great place to escape your four walls and chill out on an inclement day; kids can spot koi carp, cacti and terrapins, and everyone gets a green fix. Perhaps you could make a list of things to spot (a red flower, a cactus taller than you, a white fish) and send the kids on a ticklist scavenger hunt when you get there. Then sit back, relax and drift a little. Bliss.

Barbican Centre, Silk Street, EC2Y 8DS
barbican.org.uk/visitor-information/conservatory
020 7638 4141
FREE 🍵 ♿ 🚼
Open every other Sunday 11am–5.30pm
⊖ **Barbican, St Paul's, Moorgate**

LISTEN TO AN ART-INSPIRED STORY AT THE NATIONAL GALLERY

Every Sunday the National Gallery rolls out a magic carpet, lets it settle in front of a painting and a storyteller tells a tale inspired by that work of art. It's a brilliantly simple, calm morning event for kids aged 2–5, which provides an oh-so-gentle introduction to how to appreciate art and look at paintings in different ways.

For older kids, Family Sundays mean free art workshops. The gallery's Studio Sundays classes let 5–11-year-olds take inspiration from the works on the walls and create prints, sketches, paintings and collages, before they head to a basement studio for hands-on making. Drawing Sunday workshops (also for 5–11-year-olds) take place in the gallery itself. Both classes are led by enthusiastic, expert teachers. Places are limited, so get there nice and early.

Afterwards, we sneak into nearby Chinatown for noodles and bubble tea – try Longji on Charing Cross Road for a laid-back, café atmosphere, cheap noodles and fun, nobbly-bobbly drinks.

Trafalgar Square, WC2N 5DN
nationalgallery.org.uk/families/
020 7747 2885
FREE 🖳 ♿ 🚼

Open every day 10am–6pm. See website for workshop and storytelling times
⬤ Leicester Square, Piccadilly Circus, Charing Cross, Embankment
Buggy and wheelchair access through the Getty, Sainsbury Wing, National Café and Pigott Education Centre entrances.

WINCE WHILE YOU WATCH

THE UK COLD WATER SWIMMING CHAMPIONSHIPS

Brrrrrrrrrr! Taking part in the UK Cold Water Swimming Championships requires an ability to doggy paddle, a hardy constitution and a healthy dollop of insanity. Held at the huge and beautiful Tooting Bec Lido, this nippy biennial event (it happens on odd-numbered years) brings together experienced cold-water swimmers as well as those trying it for the first time. Dress up warmly and look smug as the hardy souls jump in. Expect short-sprint swims in all age brackets as well as a 450m-long endurance challenge for the truly weatherproof. Best of all is the hat parade and the singing of the Lido Song (there's something so antiquated and charming about that idea). Of course, there are stalls and entertainment throughout the day too. After you've got thoroughly chilled, warm up in the Bertie and Boo coffee shop (bertieandboo.com) up the road in Balham (their cakes are amazing).

Tooting Bec Road, SW16 1RU
slsc.org.uk
020 8871 7198
FREE 🚊 ♿ 🚼
Every January in odd-numbered years
⊖ Tooting Bec

The Mediatheque at the BFI is a great place to spend a wintry afternoon. The room, packed with viewing stations, is where the public can access the BFI's vast archives of films, TV programmes, public information shorts and adverts, then settle down to watch them. You simply go in, tell reception how long you'd like to stay and they'll show you to your screen, and you can browse the collection from there. There are themed collections available (retro

SNUGGLE UP WITH A CLASSIC TV SHOW
AT THE MEDIATHEQUE

children's telly treasure trove *The Kids Are Alright* is a great place to start), or create your own playlist. You can turn up on the day, but to be absolutely sure of a viewing station (especially at weekends), book in advance by telephone.

The main BFI auditorium often has family-friendly screenings on Sunday lunchtimes, so you could combine a visit to a film with a trip to the Mediatheque. Afterwards you could even treat yourselves to one of The Riverfront café's brilliant burgers.

Belvedere Road, South Bank, SE1 8XT
bfi.org.uk/archive-collections/introduction-bfi-collections/bfi-mediatheques
020 7815 1346
FREE ☕ ♿ 🚼
Open Tuesday 1pm–8pm, Wednesday–Friday 12am–8pm,
weekends 12.30pm–8pm
🚇 **Waterloo, Embankment, Charing Cross**

GET HANDS-ON

AT THE LONDON MODEL ENGINEERING EXHIBITION

Alexandra Palace's annual, huge Model Engineering Exhibition is usually held on the third weekend of January and should be marked months ahead in the calendar of any fan of tiny modes of transport. A chuffing, clacking wonderland for travel nerds of all ages, this gigantic event brings together societies and clubs, sellers and fans. Obviously, there are loads of trains in evidence, but there are many more mini modes of transport to look at. Try flying remote-controlled helicopters, hang out by the model boat pool and gasp at detailed model rockets.

Kids will absolutely adore going for rides on the bigger trains (always immensely popular, so be prepared for a bit of a queue) and there are plenty of events for really young enthusiasts. Members of the Imagineering Foundation will be on hand to answer tricky questions and inspire young engineers to greater heights. Be warned, this event may fuel a lifetime's obsession with motorised model vehicles.

Alexandra Palace Way, N22 7AY
alexandrapalace.com
020 8365 2121
££ 🎦 ♿ 🛒
Open third Friday–Sunday of January,
Friday–Saturday 10am–5pm, Sunday 10am–4.30pm,
(last entry Friday–Saturday 4pm, Sunday 3pm)
🚇 Wood Green
Food at the venue isn't hugely inspiring, so take a quick trip into Muswell Hill and visit the family-friendly Crocodile Café to refuel.

Pull on some cold-busting boots, wrap everyone up warm and get out onto the streets for London's Winter Wanders Weekend.

Walk London weekends are held four times a year and are funded by TFL. At each event there's a huge

UNCOVER THE CITY'S SECRETS ON THE WINTER WANDERS WEEKEND

series of free guided walks on offer across the capital, from leg-stretching 20k rambles to 2k strolls. Each walk has a knowledgeable guide; choose from tours of subterranean London, nature-spotting walks in some of the capital's green (or probably brown at this time of year) areas and explorations of the city's history. We like their Thames Shoreline Stroll with lots to see for easily bored kids, and gory stories of bear baiting and prisons. The Subterranean London walk explores underground London; you might discover sinister crypts, abandoned tube stations and underground rivers. Other walks take in green woodland, medieval London and a wander along the banks of the canal through Little Venice.

Older children and teenagers might like the ghost-spotting schlepps and the Millbank MI5 and MI6 tours.

- -

Across London
walklondon.org.uk
Most walks are FREE & ⚲
See website for dates and times

- -

M A K E
FANCY FROZEN ICE BALLS

Once it drops below zero outside, it's time to get crafty with ice. These mini-football-sized globes of frozen water look awesome in a front garden, or racked along a balcony. If you don't have any outside space, you can even make and stash them in a secret place in a park. It's educational too – kids learn about transformation from liquid to solids and delayed gratification – and they're very easy to do!

YOU'LL NEED

Selection of food colourings (optional)

Balloons

Water

1 Add food colouring to an empty balloon. You might want to do the next bit in the bath to avoid getting covered in water.

2 Very, very carefully and slowly, fill the balloon with water until it's stretched and as full as you can manage without it bursting. Handle it extremely gently. Knot the top.

3 Continue until you have at least as many balloons as you want ice balls (allow for some breakages).

4 Leave them outside overnight (or longer, depending on the temperature). If it has snowed, pack the snow around the balloons.

5 When the ice feels solid, snip off the balloon casing to reveal amazing, icy globes. Revel in their beauty, roll them around, play ice-bowling with them, then watch them slowly melt away.

HONE YOUR STYLE AT THE DESIGN MUSEUM

Kids go free to this stylish, sharp showcase of cutting-edge talent that's surprisingly family-friendly. Their Sunday afternoon Design and Make kids' workshops are held in a beautiful, light-filled riverside studio, and are a fantastic way to inspire a budding Jonathan Ive or Mary Katrantzou. Design-obsessed teenagers will sharpen their pencils in anticipation of the Get Into Design courses, which are led by respected names in the industry. Keep an eye out for kids-eat-free offers in the Blueprint Café above the museum.

28 Shad Thames, SE1 2YD
designmuseum.org
020 7403 6933
£££ 🍽 ♿ 🚼
Open every day 10am–5.45pm
🚇 London Bridge, Tower Hill, Tower Gateway
Adult tickets are fairly pricy, but bear in mind that under-12s get in for free.

GET OUT YOUR BINOCULARS FOR THE BIG GARDEN BIRDWATCH

The world's biggest wildlife survey, the Big Garden Birdwatch is the RSPB's annual healthcheck on the nation's avian life. It's really easy to take part; visit your local park or head into your garden for one hour and record what birds you see. Simply tot up the tweeters and pass it on to the RSPB. Easy! This survey happens every January, and there are plenty of capital-based events leading up to the event; look out for bird watches at Rainham Marshes in Essex and the London Wetland Centre (page 26) and related crafts at venues such as the Horniman Museum (page 62).

rspb.org.uk/birdwatch/
FREE
Registration for the Birdwatch is free (although you must be over 18 to sign up), and you can request a free help pack. There's also a free identification sheet to download from the RSPB's site so that you know what you're looking at!

SLEDGING IN LONDON

The rare occurrence of a snowfall in London means a beautiful, eerie silence when you wake up, days off school (if you're lucky) and, best of all, sledging. Wrap up warm and climb one of our favourite snow-strewn hills...

Alexandra Palace has plenty of speedy steep slopes to choose from, most with loads of safe braking room at the bottom. After getting chilled to the bone, we like to drink a thick, Italian-style hot chocolate from the Grove Café at the Muswell Hill end of the park.

Head up to **Primrose Hill** for views across the city and into London Zoo – it's a picturesque (if busy) place to spend an afternoon knee-deep in the white stuff.

Parliament Hill is the king of London's sledging runs, with far-reaching views and long, fast slopes. However, it's very popular and gets churned up fast. Get there first thing in the morning to avoid the crowds.

It's a long climb up the big hill in front of the Royal Observatory in **Greenwich Park**, but the view from the top is captivating. There's a fast run to the bottom, and, once you've slid down the hill (watch out for the fence), it's a short step to the National Maritime Museum's café, which serves good coffee and tummy-filling cakes.

If you want to get your speed on, **Brockwell Park** has the Cresta Run of London's sledging routes. Only for the brave!

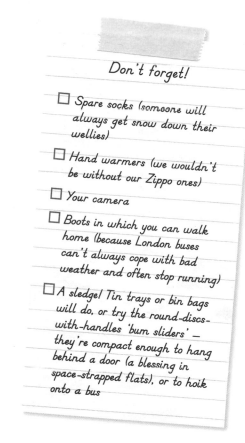

Don't forget!

☐ Spare socks (someone will always get snow down their wellies)

☐ Hand warmers (we wouldn't be without our Zippo ones)

☐ Your camera

☐ Boots in which you can walk home (because London buses can't always cope with bad weather and often stop running)

☐ A sledge! Tin trays or bin bags will do, or try the round-discs-with-handles 'bum sliders' – they're compact enough to hang behind a door (a blessing in space-strapped flats), or to hoik onto a bus

SEARCH FOR GALAXIES FAR FAR AWAY

With the long winter nights starting early in the evening, now is the prime time to look to the skies to see what planets, stars and even satellites you can spot. Why not go and stare at celestial bodies in your garden or a local park? Although the light pollution in the city makes the skies glow and the stars recede, you can get a pretty good picture in a dark park near you. (Obviously, take your safety seriously when planning this after-dark excursion.) Good places in London in which to stargaze include Epping Forest, Hampstead Heath and, of course, Greenwich Park, the home of the observatory. You'll need a night with clear skies, a big coat and torch and, if possible, a pair of binoculars or telescope. A flask of hot chocolate and a box of home-made flapjacks wouldn't go amiss too. Download an astronomy chart from *Astronomy Now*'s website (astronomynow.com), and you'll even be able to name the constellations you spot, and know what to look out for at this time of year. If you get a little more serious, why not turn up to a meeting of the family-friendly Baker Street Irregular Astronomers? The group meets each month in Regent's Park, in the heart of London, to look to the skies. They have equipment to borrow, knowledge to share and a very nice site with toilets and a café to view from.

//////////////////////////////////////

Regent's Park, NW1 4NR
bakerstreetastro.org.uk
FREE ☕ ♿ ✗
🚇 St John's Wood, Camden Town
//////////////////////////////////////

TAKE A TORCHLIT TOUR AROUND THE PETRIE MUSEUM

The Petrie Museum houses collections of Egyptian treasures that were discovered and brought back to the UK by the professors of UCL. It's an atmospheric and curious little place to visit at any time of year (because there are, like, real-life mummies in there!), but especially when it's dingy outside.

Parts of the museum are kept dark to preserve the exhibits, so visitors have to use wind-up torches to light the displays. We'd recommend teaming it with a visit to the usually-pretty-gory-or-weird Wellcome Collection just around the corner for a slightly scary, wintry day out.

Malet Place, WC1E 6BT
ucl.ac.uk/museums/petrie
020 7679 2884
FREE &♿ 🚼
Open Tuesday–Saturday 1pm–5pm
Closed over Christmas and Easter holidays
🚇 **Goodge Street, Euston Square, Warren Street**
Wheelchair and buggy lift access is available, but on very rare occasions (such as during some holidays) may not be operating. Call ahead to check.

ART AND ACTION AT BRUCE CASTLE

Haringey's Bruce Castle is an oasis plonked in the middle of bustling Tottenham. The castle houses a museum of local history and a collection of paintings, while the gardens have a fun tree trail to follow.

Their free drop-in art and craft sessions on Sunday afternoons are a great way to escape the weather and get creative on dark, wintry days. We've whiled away grim afternoons making tissue-paper lanterns, animal masks and pop-up books. The sessions are friendly and (most essentially) on every week.

If the weather is dry, try the massive adventure playground next door to burn off energy after the workshop.

Lordship Lane, N17 8NU
haringey.gov.uk/brucecastlemuseum
020 8808 8772
FREE &♿ 🚼
Open Wednesday–Sunday 1pm–5pm
Art and craft sessions Sunday at 2pm
🚇 **Wood Green, Seven Sisters**

THINGS TO DO

- ☐ Make a resolution. Learn how to tie knots, raise one eyebrow or use a washing machine (it's the resolution that keeps on giving for parents!).

- ☐ Apply for seated tickets in the stands for June's Trooping the Colour ceremony (details at royal.gov.uk).

- ☐ Head to the Geffrye Museum for their annual post-Christmas bonfire. Bye-bye holly! Bye-bye ivy! (geffrye-museum.org.uk)

- ☐ Grab your last chance to go skating around one of London's pop-up ice rinks.

- ☐ De-clutter and get creative – use old DVDs and CDs to make a garden (or balcony) mobile.

- ☐ Save energy and stay warm by making a snake-shaped draught excluder.

- ☐ Bake a Twelfth Night bean cake – hide a dried pea or bean in a regular cake; whoever gets it in their slice is crowned Bean King or Pea Queen for the year.

- ☐ It's Holocaust Memorial Day on 27 January; take the opportunity to find out more about this devastating period in modern history.

SQUEAL OVER AN OTTER ON WORLD WETLANDS DAY

World Wetlands Day gets the month off to a good start, on 2 February, aiming to raise awareness of the swampy, muddy environments loved by birds, nature and children in wellies. The London Wetland Centre in Barnes (run by the Wildfowl and Wetlands Trust) is a proper haven for wildlife that's still easily accessible from the city. Why not take a trip there to celebrate the day? We love the otter feeding and guided tours. Prices aren't dirt cheap, but you are supporting ongoing conservation work and it's a great, whole-day experience. We also love gawping at the Trust's webcams (check their website), which bring beavers, badgers and swans right onto your laptop for nothing.

Visit on a bright, sunny day (even if it is a bit chilly), as there are a lot of great outside walks and viewing platforms. Leave your best clothes at home, as there's also a fantastic playground with tunnels and a zip wire with plenty of places for adults to sit and watch their kids have fun. However, if there's a bit of unexpected drizzle, the indoor Discovery Centre is a godsend; we love the digital pond, where kids can interact and play with digitally created pool-dwelling creatures. There's also a hi-tech underwater camera that kids can operate for themselves.

Queen Elizabeth's Walk, Barnes, SW13 9WT
wwt.org.uk/visit/london/
020 8409 4400
£££ Under-4s go FREE
Open April–October 9.30am–6pm (last admission 5pm)
November–March 9.30am–5pm (last admission 4pm)
Hammersmith, Putney Bridge, Barnes
There are lots of picnic areas, so if it's a nice enough day, bring your own food.

We just love this enormous place, full of shiny vehicles and the hope of past generations. Slap-bang in the centre of town, there are stacks of well-polished cars, buses, trams and trains to peek around, historic carriages to clamber into, buttons to press and simulators to drive, plus old posters to gawp at. We are fans of the ancient tube carriages that you can sit in (with slightly scary dummies) and the fantastic, wooden, mini-TFL play table that keeps our kids occupied for at least half an hour. There are some lovely floor-projections that really tiny toddlers love to interact with, even if they have no idea of what they're all about. Get there as early as you can to avoid the crowds, and head straight for the tube-driving simulators; they always have a monster queue.

- -

Covent Garden Piazza, WC2E 7BB
ltmuseum.co.uk
020 7379 6344
£££ Under-16s go FREE ☕ ♿ 🛒
Open Monday–Thursday, Saturday and Sunday 10am–6pm, Friday 11am–6pm
🚇 **Covent Garden, Leicester Square, Holborn, Charing Cross**
Prices might seem on the steep side, but remember under-16s go free and adult tickets are good for unlimited re-admission for 12 months.

- -

DRIVE AN UNDERGROUND TRAIN AT THE LONDON TRANSPORT MUSEUM

DANCE WITH DRAGONS
AT CHINESE NEW YEAR*

Chinese New Year always makes us aware of the amazing benefits of living in multicultural London. The biggest official celebration outside Asia takes place every year in Trafalgar Square in late January or early February. It's crammed with the stuff that kids love: dragons and lions, martial arts (with sticks!), magic, firecrackers, noodles, drums and loads of people having fun (if you've got really little ones, we'd take a backpack or carrier rather than a pushchair). The parades generally start around 10am, with the main 'Dotting of the Eye' ceremony at noon in the square.

Chinatown itself is always rammed, but if you're feeling brave, explore its narrow streets and back alleys for a more authentic (and loud) experience. Try some dim sum, hear ear-splitting fireworks being let off in the street and get chased by enormous dancing dragons. Kung Hei Fat Choi!

27 Gerrard Street, W1D 6JN
chinatownlondon.org
FREE ☕ ♿ 🛒
Open every day 10am–6pm
🚇 **Charing Cross, Leicester Square, Piccadilly Circus**

COOK POTSTICKER DUMPLINGS

Makes about 40 dumplings. Halve or quarter the ingredients if you don't want as many dumplings – but you will, because they are yummy!

You'll need

pack of wonton skins (available from Chinese supermarkets – usually found in the freezer section), minimum of 40, defrosted if frozen

For the filling
220g minced pork
150g fresh spinach, finely chopped
2 tsp grated fresh ginger
2 tbsp soy sauce
1 tsp fish sauce
½ tsp ground black pepper
3 tbsp finely chopped spring onions
2 tsp sesame oil
1 tsp sugar
2 tbsp cold chicken stock or water

For the dipping sauce
3 tbsp soy sauce
1 tbsp white wine vinegar
juice ½ lime
sprinkle of chilli flakes (optional)

To cook
flour, for dusting
2 tbsp vegetable oil
150ml water

1. Put all the filling ingredients together in a bowl, mix well and put in the fridge, covered, for at least 30 minutes.

2. Combine all the dipping sauce ingredients in a small bowl and set aside.

3. Lay out the wonton skins on a lightly floured tray and place about 2 teaspoons of the filling in the centre of each skin. Dip your finger in water and lightly moisten round the edge of the skin, then fold it in half, over the filling. Pinch round the edge to seal and then pleat the edges so that the dumpling looks like a miniature Cornish pasty, flat on the bottom. Put each finished dumpling back onto the floured tray and keep them moist by covering with a clean, damp tea towel.

4. When you are ready to cook, heat a large, lidded, non-stick frying pan until hot and add half the oil (1 tablespoon). Place half the dumplings, flat side down, in the pan, reduce the heat and cook for about 2 minutes until they are lightly browned.

5. Add half the water (75ml), cover tightly with the lid and gently simmer for about 12 minutes until the water is absorbed. Check halfway through and add a little more water if they look dry. After 12 minutes, remove the lid and cook for a further 2 minutes.

6. Don't overcrowd the dumplings in the pan – cook them in more batches if your pan is small, altering the quantities of oil and water used accordingly.

7. Remove the dumplings from the pan with a slotted spoon and keep warm. Repeat until you have cooked all your dumplings.

8. As soon as they're cool enough to handle, eat them with chopsticks or pack them carefully in a lunch box to take to Chinatown. Serve them with the dipping sauce.

FUN AND FROLICS AT THE V&A MUSEUM OF CHILDHOOD*

The V&A Museum of Childhood in Bethnal Green is no dry and dusty exhibition space; it's brimming with life. We always tear up the stairs to see our giant metal pal, Robbie the Robot, who needs winding up to come alive.

Allow time to take in one of their fabulous temporary exhibitions, a workshop or a special event. Over the years we've been treated to magic lantern shows, gasped at circus performers, danced around a maypole, read poetry at an ice-cream van, scoffed jerk chicken, been taken on trips back in time in atmospheric storytelling sessions and made countless paper-based crafts. Every day there is something special happening at the venue – check the website for more details. It's an essential place for every London family to visit and make their own (local families can pretty much use it as a drop-in play centre). If you get peckish, the good-value (and award-winning) Benugo café is very kid friendly.

Cambridge Heath Road, E2 9PA
museumofchildhood.org.uk
020 8983 5200
FREE ☕ ♿ 🛒
Open every day 10am–5.45pm
🚇 **Bethnal Green**
Parents of autistic kids, nursing mothers and those in need of a serious chill-out should seek out the museum's Quiet Room on the lower ground floor. Lifesaver.

A BIT OF THE COUNTRY IN THE CORNER OF THE CITY*

London's surprisingly numerous city farms are tucked away behind railway bridges and between skyscrapers. Urban farms are great for really young city kids, who'll love meeting furry friends they know from their storybooks, while older children will start to make connections between raising animals and the food on their plates. These farms often hold special events, craft days and hands-on sessions, so check websites in advance for what's on. Here are some of our favourite.

Kentish Town City Farm

The layout is sprawling and a bit odd, but Kentish Town City Farm is one of our favourite places to take really little kids. As well as ponies to ride, ponds to dip and pigs to pat, London's oldest city farm also has a little spot in their garden dedicated to carnivorous plants! There are tiny-friendly groups galore (£) held each week, and when you get tired of the animals (like that's really going to happen) you can sit and watch the trains trundling by.

1 Cressfield Close, off Grafton Road, NW5 4BN
ktcityfarm.org.uk
020 7916 5421
FREE ♿ 🛒
Open every day 9am–5pm
🚇 **Kentish Town, Chalk Farm**

Freightliners Farm

Small but perfectly formed, Freightliners farm's friendly volunteers look after pigs, chickens, rabbits and goats. The café serves up delicious fresh food, but you're also actively encouraged to eat your packed lunches sitting in its fenced-in-and-safe area, which makes it a great destination if you're on a tight budget.

Sheringham Road, N7 8PF
freightlinersfarm.org.uk
020 7609 0467
FREE ☕ ♿ 🛒
Open Tuesday–Sunday. Autumn/Winter 10am–4pm; Spring/Summer 10am–4.45pm
🚇 **Highbury and Islington, Caledonian Road**

Mudchute Farm

With its iconic, *Emmerdale*-meets-*The Apprentice* views of Canary Wharf, this Isle of Dogs' oasis is 32 acres of peace and quiet in the heart of the financial district. We love that you can get into the sheep field and wander around, which makes it feel even more like real countryside. The excellent café is run by the same people who run the Hackney Farm and Surrey Docks farm eateries and serves delicious, locally sourced food. The farm hosts loads of great events including go-karting, dog shows and Chelsea Fringe festival events, and we like to watch the London Marathon from outside its door.

Pier Street, Isle of Dogs, E14 3HP
mudchute.org
020 7515 5901
FREE ♿ &
Open every day 9am–5pm
Mudchute, Crossharbour, Island Gardens

Deen City Farm

There's a really great range of animals at Deen City Farm, including some fine llamas, a couple of enormous pigs and an owl (great for Harry Potter fans). There's also a little riding school, and tiny jockeys-to-be will adore the Wednesday afternoon and weekend ultra-cheap taster rides around the paddock. It's part of the Morden Hall Park estate, and if you walk to the farm from Merton Abbey Mills along the river, you'll feel like you're deep in the country.

39 Windsor Avenue, Merton Abbey, SW19 2RR
deencityfarm.co.uk
020 8543 5300
FREE ♿ &
Open Tuesday–Sunday and Bank Holiday Mondays 10am–4.30pm
Colliers Wood, South Wimbledon

Spitalfields City Farm

Set up in the 1970s, the Spitalfields City Farm nestles in the heart of east London, and is a real community hub. There are donkeys, goats, pigs (we always check in on Holmes and Watson) and a garden run by passionate volunteers. Plus a really great treehouse for kids to hang out in. Enjoy the live music and stalls at their regular festivals, such as the Strawberry and Honey Fayre and Cowfest, but the highlight of their calendar is the annual Oxford vs Cambridge Goat Race (£), which takes place on the same day as its water-based almost-namesake (page 57). They also run an excellent weekly Saturday play project where 8–13-year-olds can learn to care for animals, ride donkeys, do some gardening and take part in arts and crafts sessions (£).

Buxton Street, E1 5AR
spitalfieldscityfarm.org
020 7247 8762
FREE &
Open Tuesday–Sunday 10am–4.30pm
Whitechapel, Shoreditch High Street, Aldgate East, Bethnal Green

MAKE A LOVEBIRD MOBILE

Decorate your children's bedroom with hearts and lovebirds ready for Valentine's Day. Older kids will love to make the birds themselves, and younger ones will adore helping to tie the decorations onto the branch.

YOU'LL NEED

Pen

Scraps of felt or fabric

Scissors

Needle and thread

Beads/sequins/ feathers/shells, to decorate

Cotton wool

Ribbon

Branch/stick/ coathanger

1 Draw a simple bird shape on whatever material you are using, and cut out four identical pieces.

2 Decorate each piece with stitching, beads or whatever you have (make sure to flip every other one so that the decoration is on the correct side).

3 Stitch each bird together, leaving a little gap at the top, then stuff with cotton wool. Stitch up the gap once filled. Use the same technique to make a heart.

4 Sew a loop of ribbon onto each item, and hang them up on a branch, stick or coathanger.

SHARE STORIES AT THE LONDON CHILDREN'S BOOK SWAP

Most families have old books knocking around that they don't really read or need any more. And we're always looking for new stories to add to the bedtime read. So three cheers that every February you can exchange your tired tomes for something new at the London Children's Book Swap, the brainchild of the London Discover Children's Story Centre (page 56).

The event runs at multiple venues across the city, from arts centres to theatres and libraries. Participating locations include artsdepot (page 213), Rich Mix (page 164), the Ministry of Stories in East London (ministryofstories.org), and the Barbican (page 181). Just bring a bag of your old books and swap each of them for a new-to-you read.

There are also related events including illustration workshops, crafts and even free boat trips.

Across London
worldbookday.com
01634 729 810
FREE
See website for event details, dates and times

LET YOUR IMAGINATION RUN

WILD

AT THE IMAGINE CHILDREN'S FESTIVAL*

Every year, over the spring half-term holiday, the Southbank Centre hosts a fun-packed series of events geared totally around kids' literature and performing arts. There are shows, live bands and lots of book-related activities (there are over 60 separate events taking place over the week-and-a-bit festival). We especially love the free art workshops led by children's illustrators (our lot adored the pop-up-book-making class they attended), the truly ground-breaking interactive theatre events and super-special author readings.

As well as paid-for shows and classes, there's tons of free stuff happening. Maybe you'll stumble across a dinosaur-petting zoo, a bicycle-powered disco or an opera for babies. If it all gets too much, there's a parenting room on Level 2 for quiet time and breastfeeding. Tiny bums will appreciate the small toilets on the Spirit Level at the Royal Festival Hall.

Belvedere Road, SE1 8XX
southbankcentre.co.uk
020 7960 4200
FREE–£££ ☕ ♿ 🛒
Open spring half-term (check the website for dates)
Ⓣ **Waterloo, Embankment, Charing Cross**
There's a great selection of chain cafés around the Southbank complex; our kids absolutely adore Wagamama and Giraffe, but you're also more than welcome to bring your own food and eat it at the tables in the foyer spaces.

PEEP BEHIND THE SCENES AT THE NATIONAL THEATRE

Got a child obsessed with the theatre or dying to take to the stage? Get a real insight into the day-to-day workings of one of the city's premier venues with a backstage tour of the National Theatre.

The tours run all day, every day and there are specially constructed gantries and access points so that you can get closer to the action. During half-term and holidays, the tours are even more family friendly, and you can handle props and even try on real costumes. On selected Saturdays, there are tours that take in more of the costume-making process. It's best to book ahead, and bear in mind that children under five are not permitted on the visits.

South Bank, SE1 9PX
nationaltheatre.org.uk/discover/backstage-tours
020 7452 3000
££ **(up to** three 5–12-year-olds go FREE **with every adult on the family tours)** 🚊 ♿
Open Monday–Friday: 10.15am, 10.30am, 12.15pm, 12.30pm, 5.15pm, 5.30pm; Saturday: 10.30am and 12.15pm; Sunday: 12.30pm (on days when the building is open); call 020 7452 3400 to check timings of tours
🚇 **Waterloo, Southwark, Embankment**
Use your tour ticket to get money off in the NT's coffee shop and bookstore.

EXPERIENCE AN EARTHQUAKE AT THE NATURAL HISTORY MUSEUM*

Of course, you'll want to take in the enormous, animatronic Tyrannosaurus Rex, the reproduction dino-skeletons and gargantuan blue whale, but, as ever with the bigger museums, it's worth heading off the beaten track to get away from the crowds and uncover some gems.

We love the Investigate Centre on the lower ground floor; it has free timed entry but it's never too crowded, and there are hands-on specimens with microscopes, scales and enough measuring and investigating equipment to satisfy the most curious of tiny minds.

Other must-sees include the earthquake machine in the Red Zone, the mesmerising quadrasphere installation in the Ecology Gallery (a great sensory experience for really little kids) and the giant moving scorpion model in the Creepy Crawlies gallery. There are always new temporary exhibitions popping up (we're fans of the butterfly tent that appears on the huge front lawn most summers) and loads of kid-orientated special events. Younger children will love the museum's regular puppet shows, which tell a story while teaching nippers about science, and the chance to handle live specimens. The Attenborough Studio in the museum shows free films every day offering a bit of respite from the hurly-burly of the main floor.

Our top tip is to take one of the free behind-the-scenes tours of the Darwin Centre's Spirit Collection (which includes a chance to see an enormous, preserved giant squid). They are unmissable for those over eight, and a chance to take a peek into the endless corridors and rooms full of jars of specimens, including preserved beasts found by Darwin himself.

Cromwell Road, SW7 5BD
nhm.ac.uk
020 7942 5000
FREE 🚼 ♿ ✈
Open every day 10am–5.50pm, last Friday of every month 10am–10.30pm
🚇 **South Kensington**
Use the entrance on Exhibition Road to get in; there are much smaller (often non-existent) queues there, plus a ramp for buggies and wheelchairs, and a generally more chilled start to your big trip.

CHUCKLE IN THE AISLES
AT THE CLOWNS' CHURCH SERVICE

If you're nervous around clowns, be sure to avoid east London on the first Sunday in February. But if you like red-nosed revellers, put your huge shoes on and prepare to chuckle. The annual Clowns' Church Service takes place at Holy Trinity Church in Dalston, as hundreds of painted men and ladies come together for a memorial service for the greatest clown of all, Grimaldi. Space in the church is very limited, so arrive early or just stand outside for the spectacle. Make sure to have a look at the little corner of the church dedicated to circus memorabilia after the event.

The service is followed by a clown show for kids in the church hall.

Beechwood Road, E8 3DY
trinitysaintsunited.com
020 7254 5062
FREE ♿ 🛒
Service held first Sunday in February, 3pm
Dalston Kingsland

MAKE
PANCAKE DAY
FLIPPING
FANTASTIC

Pancake Day is one of our favourite festivals. Why? Because it's all about the *eating*. London hosts some great annual events to mark Shrove Tuesday; watch crazily dressed teams flip their pancakes in Spitalfields, or head over the river to see how they do it in the south at Bankside. Meanwhile, Greenwich Market has some more ambitious events, including a children's race (it's always more fun if you can join in).

If you'd rather eat your pancakes than flip them, there are plenty of places to grab a stack in London, but you'll need to book well ahead for a Pancake Day seat. We love The Breakfast Club's, especially when they come with bacon and maple syrup (thebreakfastclubcafes.com), My Old Dutch (myolddutch.com) and the batter-meisters at Crepe Affaire (crepeaffaire.com) for take-away or café-style eat-in.

Great Spitafields Pancake Race
Old Truman Brewery, 91 Brick Lane, Spitafileds, E1 6QL
alternativearts.co.uk
020 7375 0441
FREE
Shoreditch High Street

THINGS TO DO

FEBRUARY

☐ Go on a London safari — see how many statues and pictures of wild beasts you can spot on a walk through the city.

☐ Search for catkins in your local park.

☐ There are big, juicy lemons in the greengrocers now, so make a lemon drizzle cake.

☐ Go for a trip to the Twinings Tea Shop and museum at 216 Strand, then teach your kids to make a proper cup of tea (an essential life-skill!).

☐ Rediscover the magic of making things up or reading aloud during National Storytelling Week.

☐ Write a Valentine's Day poem together.

☐ Enter the Open Garden Square Weekend's ballot to get tickets to the city's most prestigious gardens (page 99).

☐ Check out what plays will be performed outside this summer (look at Regent's Park Open Air Theatre for a start) and book tickets.

☐ Go to the funfair that takes place on Clapham Common every February half-term.

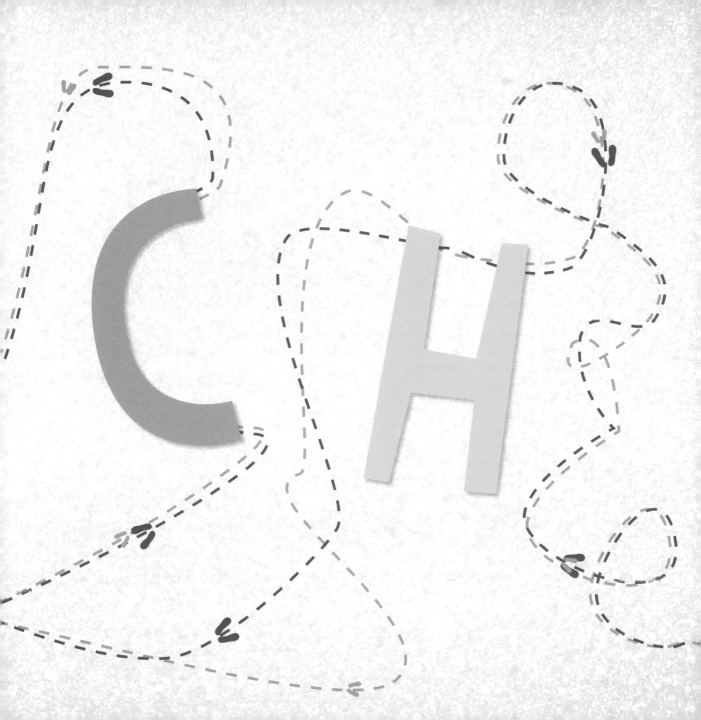

SIT UP STRAIGHT AT THE RAGGED SCHOOL

You might think that on a Sunday a strict classroom is the last place your kids would want to be, but our older, less sensitive children love taking part in the Victorian-style lessons.

Led by a very stern teacher (don't worry, corporal punishment isn't on the curriculum), kids (and adults) are led through a typical education experience, complete with old desks, slates, inkwells, dunce caps and lots of over-acting.

Afterwards, you'll have the chance to handle historic objects in the Victorian kitchen, or return, thankfully, to modern times with a cup of tea in the exceptionally good-value café (which sells small snacks, but not much more, so bring your own sandwiches). Open House day runs on the first Sunday of every month.

46–50 Copperfield Road, E3 4RR
raggedschoolmuseum.org.uk
020 8980 6405
FREE (with a small donation) 🏷
Open Wednesday–Thursday 10am–5pm
Open days on the first Sunday of every month, 2pm–5pm, lessons at 2.15pm and 3.30pm
🚇 **Mile End**
No wheelchair access beyond the ground floor.

ENTER A WORLD OF ART, MUSIC AND DRAMA AT THE TELEGRAPH HILL FESTIVAL

Often it's the smaller-scale festivals in London that are the most fun. Run by volunteers, the Telegraph Hill festival is jam-packed with child-friendly, lo-fi events that are an absolute blast. Perhaps you'll hop on an old Routemaster bus for an art exhibition, take in a free storytelling session, go for a 'bark in the park' with some friendly pooches, find some tasty wild food on a foraging walk or learn the art of knitting at a workshop. It runs every year for three weekends from the beginning of March.

102a Pepys Road, New Cross Gate, SE14 5TY
telegraphhillfestival.org.uk
FREE ♿ 🚼
🚇 **New Cross Gate, Brockley**

CELEBRATE HOLI AT ORLEANS HOUSE GALLERY

The serene and ornate Orleans House Gallery is set in idyllic wooded gardens right next to the river. Alongside their eclectic art exhibitions they run free drop-in workshops (2pm–4.30pm) on the first Sunday of each month. There's also a monthly Saturday art class that's a little more immersive, and is designed for single parents or carers who are alone with their children at weekends.

The gallery holds regular celebrations, including a party in March to celebrate the Hindu festival of Holi, where families are entertained by Bollywood dancing and music and fling rainbow-coloured powders at each other.

If all that hurling and creativity makes you hungry, grab a booth at the café that's housed in the old stables.

Riverside, Twickenham TW1 3DJ

richmond.gov.uk/home/leisure_and_culture/arts/orleans_house_gallery

020 8831 6000

FREE 🍴 ♿ 🛒

Open Tuesday–Saturday 1pm–4.30pm (5.30pm April–September), Sunday and Bank Holidays 2pm–4.30pm (5.30pm April–September)

🚇 St Margarets

If you don't live near the gallery, why not take the TFL River Bus up the Thames for a day trip? Change at Hampton Court for the Richmond boat.

CREATE A HILARIOUS FAMILY PORTRAIT AT THE BRITISH MUSEUM

Let's face it, everyone loves the mummies. There hasn't been a Hopscotch trip to the British Museum that hasn't involved peering in horror at the dried-out bodies of cats, dogs and humans in the Egyptian galleries. But there's loads more to the British Museum.

The gigantic Elgin Marbles galleries fascinate pushchair-bound babies, and there are huge Day of the Dead models and Easter Island statues to gawp at, the Lindow Man to examine and golden treasures and jewellery to pore over. We always try to take in the clock gallery, which includes an astonishing mechanical galleon designed to sail across a table firing cannon and playing music. There are also loads of opportunities to handle objects from the museum's collection; check in advance where the exploration tables are situated on the day of your visit, or ask at the information desk.

However, the museum certainly isn't stuck in the past. Every weekend, the Samsung Digital Centre is thronged with kids taking part in workshops using cutting-edge technology.

One week, you might be able to take part in a 'virtual autopsy' of a mummy, another to make a manga comic using images of objects from the museum, or perhaps create a picture of you and your family interacting with treasures from the galleries.

Great Russell Street, WC1B 3DG
britishmuseum.org
020 7323 8299
FREE ☕ ♿ ⛴
Open every day 10am–5.30pm, except Fridays 10am–8.30pm
🚇 **Tottenham Court Road, Holborn, Russell Square, Goode Street**
Under-12s eat free all day with an adult in the Gallery Café.

SEE THE FINEST FLYING MACHINES AT THE RAF MUSEUM*

Our top-secret, excess-energy-burn-off haven is the free RAF Museum in Colindale, North London, which is an unsung paradise for kids. Because of its location and ENORMOUS size (the hulking aeroplanes are housed in massive hangars), it rarely gets too crowded, and the gigantic collection of flying machines will awe even the most jaded sky-watcher.

Throw in a spectacular Battle of Britain and Blitz lightshow, flight simulators (£) and a 4D cinema (£) and your nippers will be loop-the-loop with excitement. Really little kids will just love running around the huge spaces, dwarfed by the fighter planes and cargo carriers.

There are stacks of special events, including visits from birds of prey, arts and crafts sessions and a great interactive kids section with mini-aeroplanes to pilot, a hang-glider to swing from and buttons to push. There are two excellent cafés on site, with the Wings Restaurant being particularly kid friendly. There are also indoor and outdoor picnic areas.

Grahame Park Way, NW9 5LL
rafmuseum.org.uk
020 8205 2266
FREE 🚊 ♿ 🚻
Open every day 10am–6pm (10am–5pm November–February)
🚇 Colindale
If you're going by car, use the museum's street address rather than postcode in your satnav, or you may be directed onto the hard shoulder of the M1 (yes, this happened to us)!

EAT LIKE A VICTORIAN
AT VALENTINES MANSION

Tucked away between Gants Hill underground and Ilford station, Valentines Mansion and Gardens is a cute little hidden gem of a place to visit. Open February to October, the 300-year-old house and grounds is a lovely place to explore with kids; nose around the Victorian kitchen, where it really does seem that the cook's just stepped out of the door, poke into the walled garden and run around the park (see if you can find the little grottos). And remember to go and look for the tortoises in the cottage garden – they should start waking from hibernation about now.

There are absolutely loads of kid-friendly things to see and do. Dress up in Victorian costumes, rustle up a pretend feast in a play kitchen, make a mini-mansion in an art class or settle down to a storytelling session.

Check the website for special events including workshops, gardening afternoons and history explorer days.

Emerson Road, Ilford, Essex, IG1 4XA
valentinesmansion.com
020 8708 8100
FREE 🍵 ♿ 🚼

Open February and October, Tuesdays (October only) and Sundays 11am–3pm; March–September, Tuesdays 10am–5pm and Sundays 11am–5pm (closed November–January apart from special events)

🚇 **Gants Hill, Ilford**

DANCE A JIG ON ST PATRICK'S DAY

St Patrick's Day is generally more of an adult occasion across the capital; an excuse for office workers to down pints of Guinness and wear a stupid green hat. But the celebration in Trafalgar Square on the nearest Sunday to the date every year is decidedly family-orientated and attracts over 100,000 people. The fun starts at noon with a huge parade of bands, massive model animals, dancers and floats that represent each county of Ireland.

The celebrations continue in the Square with bands, comedians, dancing and a children's tent where kids can make Irish-themed knick-knacks, listen to stories and learn how to jig or play Gaelic football. Trafalgar Square springs to life on days like these, becoming a focal point for London's myriad communities who come together to share their different cultures.

Trafalgar Square, WC2N 5DN
london.gov.uk/events
FREE 🚇 ♿ 👶
Open 12pm–6pm. Parade starts at Piccadilly, by Green Park, at 12pm
🚇 Leicester Square, Piccadilly Circus, Charing Cross, Embankment

Alternatively!

Make your way to Camden's Irish Centre, which holds a whole weekend of events to celebrate the country's patron saint, including family céilís, craft sessions and concerts. There are always massive pots of traditional Irish grub cooking away somewhere in the building. Don't forget to wear green!

50–52 Camden Square, NW1 9XB
londonirishcentre.org
FREE–£££ 🚇 ♿ 👶
Open Friday 7.30pm–late, Saturday 12pm–late, Sunday 9am–late
🚇 Camden Town

EXPERIENCE LIFE ON BOARD HMS BELFAST

Some big tourist attractions in London are a bit of a let-down, but HMS *Belfast* won't disappoint. A ship moored in the centre of town – that's an immersive experience.

Rather than reading about how it feels to work on board a war ship, kids actually feel it; the cramped surroundings, low ceilings, small bunks and huge engines, there are even authentic smells. Eeeew! The gun turret experience further enhances the authenticity, with lights, vibrations and sounds that all recreate how it would have felt to be a sailor on the ship in 1943. The mannequins can be slightly scary for younger kids and there are some really steep steps, so make sure everyone's in their trainers.

Be sure to take the free family audio tour, with the recollections of sailors who served on the ship. The onboard Walrus Café is great for posh sandwiches and toasties.

The Queen's Walk, SE1 2JH
iwm.org.uk/visits/hms-belfast
020 7940 6300
£££ Under-16s FREE 🚆 ♿ 🚼
Open November–February 10am–5pm (last admission 4pm);
March–October 10am–6pm (last admission 5pm)
🚇 **London Bridge, Tower Hill**
Mostly accessible to wheelchair and buggy users,
but some areas inaccessible. No cloakroom.

HUNT FOR FROGSPAWN AT GREENWICH PENINSULA PARK

It's that time of year when ponds across the capital transform into writhing pits of amphibians and weird jelly-like spawn fills our boating lakes. It's almost tadpole season! Greenwich Peninsula Ecology Park makes amphibian-spawning even more fun at their yearly Frog Day (held on the second Sunday in the month). The free event includes a chance to make froggy art, do some pond dipping, look at eggs under a microscope, follow prize trails and browse gift stalls. Plus there's usually someone wandering around in a giant frog costume.

The park is a great place to visit all year, with pond dipping and bug hunting every Wednesday and other family activities taking place during the summer holidays. There are bird hides to peer out at geese and lots of bogs to poke around in. Heaven.

Thames Path, John Harrison Way, SE10 0QZ
urbanecology.org.uk
020 8293 1904
FREE 🚆 ♿ 🚼
Open Wednesday–Sunday 10am–5.30pm or dusk, whichever
comes first; closed over Christmas and New Year
🚇 **North Greenwich**

TAKE A SONIC TRAIL AT TATE MODERN

Tate Modern is one of our favourite places to visit with kids and is especially good on cold and rainy days. It's not the kind of place where kids get angrily shushed, and the art is weird enough to totally entrance children. Make things even more fun by taking out one of their Sonic Trail headphones and getting a wildly different, nipper-friendly perspective on the gallery. Or grab a set of the museum's coloured filters that are especially designed for kids; peering through the rainbow-coloured glasses will give them a whole new perspective on the art on show and the building's architecture. They're free to borrow from the information desks on levels 0 and 1.

If you'd rather get hands-on, the venue's free Open Studio has a wealth of materials to create your own artworks related to the exhibitions, and is open every weekend and Thursdays and Fridays in school holidays, 11am–4pm. Keep an eye out on the venue's website for one-off, teen-and-kid-friendly festivals too.

Bankside, SE1 9TG
tate.org.uk/visit/tate-modern
020 7887 8888
FREE 🖼 ♿ 🛒
Open Sunday–Thursday 10am–6pm, Friday–Saturday 10am–10pm
🚇 **Southwark, Blackfriars, St Paul's**
Look out for great offers in the excellent café on Level 1 – for example, at lunchtimes, kids eat for free when an accompanying adult buys a main course.

SHOUT 'AYE, AYE CAPTAIN!'
AT THE MARITIME MUSEUM

This magnificient building houses a collection of seafaring-related objects and wonders, including the new, interactive installation, The Great Map, over which you can walk and find out about the real-time movements of ships around the world.

The Children's Gallery includes a shoot-a-pirate-ship giant game, a galley where you can help prepare food for sailors and the explorable ship, *Seahorse*. Older kids will absolutely love the huge ship simulator; there's a variety of really tough challenges that are enormous fun.

Other treasures on display include a real-life pirate's sword, Nelson's jacket (complete with bullet-hole and blood) and the world's biggest ship-in-a-bottle.

Every Saturday a maritime character is brought to life for storytelling sessions, and weekly Sunday workshops include craft and discovery events. There are also regular theme days and parties that take place across the museum and its grounds. Make a day of it by combining your visit with a trip to the nearby Cutty Sark or Greenwich Observatory, or take the opportunity for a wander around the lovely Greenwich Market.

— —— — —— — — —— — —— — —— — —— — — ·

Romney Road, Greenwich, SE10 9NF
rmg.co.uk
020 8858 4422
FREE 🚻 ♿ 🚼
**Open every day 10am–5pm (last admission 4.30pm),
except Thursday 10am–8pm**
🚇 **Cutty Sark, Greenwich**

— —— — —— — — —— — —— — —— — —— — — ·

WATCH THE CITY GO DARK FOR EARTH HOUR

Held on a Saturday towards the end of March, during WWF's Earth Hour (earthhour.org), people all over the world turn off their lights not only to save electricity, but to make a dynamic, unified statement about respecting the Earth and protecting its resources.

At 8.30pm, homes, businesses and iconic buildings, including the Eiffel Tower and Sydney Opera House, spend 60 minutes lamp-free to raise awareness of renewable energy. While lights-out may fall before 8.30pm for your little ones, it's still a good chance to get them thinking about the impact of what we consume every day. If you want to fire up your kids' enthusiasm for going green, why not visit the Natural History Museum's great Ecology exhibit (page 38).

You could even learn more about protest and green lifestyles by heading to Transition Heathrow (a squatted, off-grid community garden) for one of their gardening Sundays or Saturday Crafternoons. You'll meet full-time protestors as well as learn about gardening basics and off-grid living in an old plant nursery. They're a friendly bunch, and kids will get a great introduction to green lifestyles and peaceful protesting.

Grow Heathrow, Vineries Close, Sipson, West Drayton, UB7 0JH
transitionheathrow.com
07890 751 568
FREE 📷 ♿ 🐾

Open Monday–Saturday 10am–6pm, Sunday 2pm–6pm
⊖ **Hounslow West**

ZOOM ACROSS THE THAMES ON THE EMIRATES AIR LINE

This cable car route stretching across the Thames from Docklands (near the ExCeL centre) to the Greenwich Peninsula was opened just before the London Olympics in 2012. It's a great way to get a bargain white-knuckle experience, complete with some of the most spectacular views in London. Go on a clear day and you'll see the financial district glistening in front of you as you sway across the Thames.

It's a lovely way to get across the river, and with the O2 Centre, the Greenwich Peninsula Ecology Park (page 50), the ExCeL Centre and the Thames Barrier Park all within striking distance of the terminals, you can make a proper day out of your trip.

Royal Docks terminal, 27 Western Gateway, E16 1FA
Greenwich Peninsula terminal, Edmund Halley Way, SE10 0FR
emiratesairline.co.uk
0843 222 1234
££ Under-5s go FREE ♿ ⛟
Open summer (1 April–30 September) Monday to Friday 7am–9pm, Saturday 8am–9pm, Sunday 9am–9pm; winter (1 October–31 March) Monday to Friday 7am–8pm, Saturday 8am–8pm, Sunday 9am–8pm
🚇 Royal Victoria, North Greenwich
Go at an off-peak time when the queues are shorter and the cars are slowed down; more ride for your money! Cheaper with an Oyster card too.

BE ENCHANTED AT THE DISCOVER STORY CENTRE

The Discover Children's Story Centre in Stratford is a magical place for young kids, gently exploring their imaginations and encouraging them into a lifetime's love of reading. As well as top children's authors appearing for chats, classes and signings weekly, there is usually an interactive exhibition or show in the Story Studio (the hugely popular Christmas show *The House Where Winter Lives* was a firm favourite of ours). The indoor and outdoor story trails are permanent, with wonders to explore that include a space rocket, a huge pirate ship, gigantic musical instruments, loads of costumes to dress up in and things to make.

We adore the place; it's small enough that you can let your kids run around without worrying about them getting lost. Go for one of their special events or turn up on a quieter day for a leisurely play. It's really near Westfield Stratford, so is a great place to recover your senses after a shopping trip, or for some members of the family to enjoy while others go mental in the mall.

383–387 High Street, Stratford, E15 4QZ
discover.org.uk
020 8536 5555
£ Under-2s go FREE 🍴 ♿ 🚼
Open Tuesday–Friday 10am–5pm, Saturday and Sunday 11am–5pm
🚇 Stratford
Newham residents get a discount on the entry price.

CHEER ON YOUR FAVOURITE

AT THE OXFORD vs CAMBRIDGE BOAT (AND GOAT) RACE

The Oxford vs Cambridge boat race is (usually) a sign that spring is here. But whatever the temperatures, you'll have fun.

You'll have to get to the prime spots on the river's edge early to get a good view, but if you don't fancy standing around in the (possibly) freezing cold waiting for the crews to flash past, bag a place in front of the big screens in Bishop's Park or Furnivall Gardens. There's entertainment, plus refreshments and children's rides.

However, we always prefer to head to the Oxford vs Cambridge *Goat* Race. It's even more exciting (and much cuter) than its more glamorous, water-based inspiration. Held at Spitalfields Farm as a fundraiser, two horned challengers represent the colleges, and go head-to-head in a race from their paddock to the feeding area. It's very funny, there's plenty more entertainment on hand and it's totally animal friendly.

theboatrace.org
FREE ♿ 🚼
Open 12pm–5pm, race time depends on tide
⊖ Putney Bridge, Hammersmith

Buxton Street, E1 5AR
spitalfieldscityfarm.org
020 7247 8762
£ ♿ 🚼
Open 1pm, race starts at the same time as the river race
⊖ Whitechapel, Shoreditch High Street, Aldgate East, Bethnal Green

EXPLORE AN OLYMPIC ADVENTURE PLAYGROUND

We were so sad when the 2012 Olympics came to an end, but there's a little corner of London where the dream lives on. Queen Elizabeth Olympic Park was the site of the games, but now instead of athletes breaking records, kids are running wild. The park is an enormous green space intersected by cycle paths, rivers and ponds. There's a brilliant, nature-inspired playground with dens, bug-hunting areas and pods hung high in trees with views across the park, and an extremely fairly priced, but still absolutely delicious, social-enterprise café next door.

The park is gradually opening to the public once more, offering trips up Anish Kapoor's iconic Orbit tower (the viewing platform is 80m high) (£££), so visitors can look out across East London and beyond, and access to the Velodrome for bicycle training for cyclists of all abilities.

//////////////////////////////////////

E20 2ST
queenelizabetholympicpark.co.uk
0800 072 2110
FREE 🍽 ♿ 🚼
Open summer 6am–10pm, winter 6am–7pm
🚇 **Hackney Wick, Stratford**
\\\

THINGS TO DO

MARCH

☐ Check for early bird tickets for summer family festivals (we like Lollibop, which takes place in August, and features appearances from kids' TV icons) – buy them early and get them cheap!

☐ Go foraging for wild garlic.

☐ Mark International Women's Day by talking about inspirational female friends or relatives.

☐ Find out if there's a community garden near you that runs kids' gardening events.

☐ Welcome back the sun at the Russian festival of Maslenitsa in Trafalgar Square (maslenitsa.co.uk).

☐ Start planning your Big Lunch (page 101).

☐ Celebrate National Science and Engineering Week (check britishscienceassociation.org for events near you).

☐ Try out a new instrument for free on Learn To Play Day (learntoplayday.com).

☐ Find some blossom and snap some cheery pictures.

☐ Make something beautiful for Mother's Day.

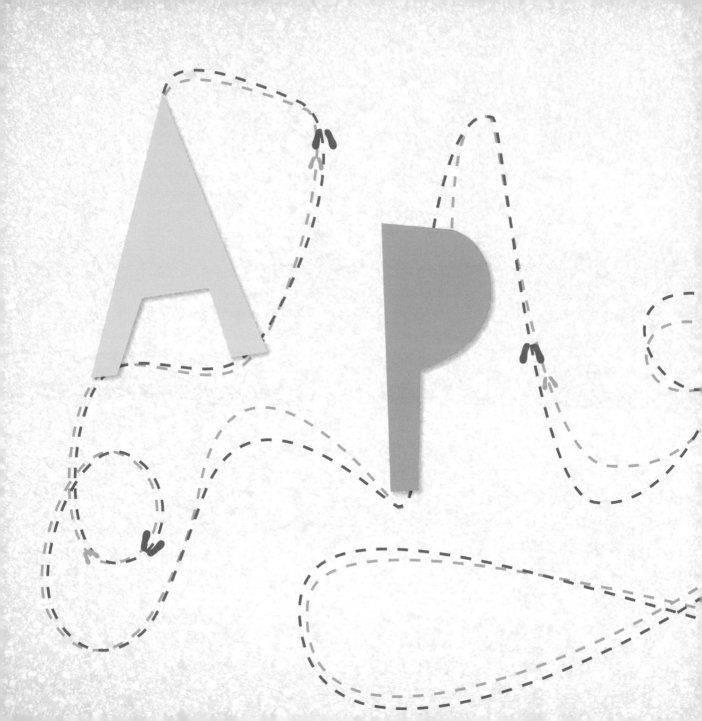

FEEL LIKE AN EXPLORER AT THE HORNIMAN MUSEUM*

One of our favourite places to hang out with our kids, the Horniman Museum is a truly magnificent building, with a wonderful conservatory, set in 16 acres of parkland.

It's a wonderland for kids, where ancient artefacts are displayed in nipper-friendly and often very modern ways. Our lot love to go and say hello to the totem pole outside the main entrance, then on to the gigantic stuffed walrus in the Natural History Gallery and, last of all, take in the neon-bright fish in the colourful aquarium (£).

There are stacks of hands-on exhibits like Native American headdresses and Indonesian tribal masks to play with, and buttons to press that will keep little hands busy and little minds entertained.

The gardens are perfect for a wander on a warm spring day, and there are even a few rabbits and goats to pet. Every weekend (and through the holidays) the museum hosts a slew of great events for kids, from storytelling sessions to craft workshops. We're fans of their Spring Trails and Welly Walks, which take you on guided explorations of the gardens to find the first green shoots of spring, and often a few beasties.

----

100 London Road, Forest Hill, SE23 3PQ
horniman.ac.uk
020 8699 1872
FREE (workshops £, aquarium £, bigger exhibitions £) 🚊 ♿ ✕
Open every day 10.30am–5.30pm
⊖ Forest Hill
The Horniman's Youth Panel is a very active volunteer group for teenagers. Join up to help put on cool events and have your say in the running of the museum.

FLAT CAPS, PIPES AND VINTAGE BIKES AT THE LONDON TWEED RUN

Every year, hundreds of retro-spectacular gents and ladies don their best capes, hats and knickerbockers, jump on their bicycles and take part in the Annual Tweed Run. It's a nod to a golden age of cycling, with pipes and picnic baskets as far as the eye can see. Kids will love gawping at the eccentric parade, and might even be inspired to travel more on two wheels rather than four.

The cycle starts at Marylebone High Street, then on to Regent Street, Savile Row and Piccadilly Circus. It then trundles along past the Houses of Parliament before doubling back to Trafalgar Square. Although Savile Row seems most appropriate, we recommend watching the riders come into Trafalgar Square.

tweedrun.com
FREE
See the website for dates and times

GET INTO DESIGN AT PICK ME UP

Today's kids are fascinated by graphic design. It's a constant in their lives – they're surrounded by ads, logos are more important than ever, cartoons are the most popular shows on kids TV and even choosing a font to use on their laptop is a life-or-death decision. Pick Me Up is a massive, annual graphic arts festival at Somerset House (page 98), which is aimed as much at kids as at design dudes with thick-rimmed glasses and fixed-gear bikes.

There are always amazing children's workshops from which to pick and choose. In the past they've held events with Aardman modelmaker Jim Parkyn and Gruffalo creator Axel Scheffler, and other activities have included a tattoo-designing class (don't worry, none of the ink was permanent) and a chance to doodle on walls. Perfect for little hipsters and their design-loving parents.

Strand, WC2R 1LA
pickmeuplondon.com
020 3565 6557
££ ▣ & 🚻
Open every day 10am–6pm, except Thursday 10am–10pm (last entry 5.15pm, Thursday 9.15pm, depending on gallery)
⊖ Temple, Covent Garden, Charing Cross, Embankment

VISIT HERITAGE HOMES ON THE NATIONAL TRUST FREE WEEKEND

Each year, for one weekend during March or April, the National Trust creaks open some very old doors to the public and offers free entry for everyone.

London has some real treasures to explore. **Sutton House** is an atmospheric Tudor building in the heart of East London, with carved fireplaces, oak panelling and even a mural left by 1980s squatters. Its hip location means that there are often wonderfully arty events taking place within its walls, such as collaborations with artist Gavin Turk's *House of Fairy Tales*, creators of fantasy worlds for children or a crafty carnival day.

More boisterous kids may prefer 17th-century **Ham House**'s smorgasbord of activities. Pick from a garden trail or an indoor voyager hunt, themed art activities in the basement or getting hands-on in the kitchen. (Older kids may be more interested in the fact that the building is a regular in the *Horrible Histories* TV programme. When you've worn yourself out, grab a cup of tea at the Orangery Café while the kids muck about on the play equipment in the kitchen garden.

However, our favourite National Trust-related activity is to keep things simple, and take advantage of their beautiful green spaces.

A great place for south Londoners to fill their lungs with clean air, **Morden Hall Park** has the River Wandle flowing through it, a series of crumbly old buildings to explore, acres of lush, natural space and a natural play area for energetic kids. Blooming blissful, if you ask us.

Sutton House
2 and 4 Homerton High Street, Hackney, E9 6JQ
nationaltrust.org.uk/sutton-house-and-breakers-yard/
020 8986 2264
FREE ☕ ♿ 🚼
See website for dates and times
🚇 Hackney Central

Ham House
Ham Street, Ham, Richmond-upon-Thames, TW10 7RS
nationaltrust.org.uk/ham-house/
020 8940 1950
££ ☕ ♿ 🚼
See website for dates and times
🚇 Richmond

Morden Hall Park
Morden Hall Road, Morden, SM4 5JD
nationaltrust.org.uk/morden-hall-park/
020 8545 6850
FREE ☕ ♿ 🚼
See website for dates and times
🚇 Morden

LAUGH AT A JESTER
ON ST GEORGE'S DAY

St George's Day is a chance to celebrate the richness of our country's past and welcome a multicultural, inclusive future.

On the Saturday nearest the 25th, Trafalgar Square will be buzzing with life, with free food tastings, music and quirky events (we loved 2012's pop-up gardens that covered the concourse and 2013's dragon-training school). Kids will love the theatre shows, jugglers and jesters, plus be sure to head to the children's area for craft workshops and storytelling.

If you can't face the crowds of central London, Bethnal Green's V&A Museum of Childhood also usually hosts a more low-key celebration of the day, with country dancing, games and Punch and Judy shows.

Trafalgar Square, WC2N 5DN
london.gov.uk/events
FREE 🍽 ♿ 🚼
Open 12pm–6pm
🚇 Leicester Square, Piccadilly Circus, Charing Cross, Embankment

Cambridge Heath Road, E2 9PA
museumofchildhood.org.uk
020 8983 5200
FREE 🍽 ♿ 🚼
Open every day 10am–5.45pm
🚇 Bethnal Green

CLIMB UP BRIXTON WINDMILL

We love stumbling across secret corners of London, and one thing you wouldn't expect to find is a working windmill in the middle of Brixton, but it's there all right. It's open for free tours to the public on weekends from April, and throughout the spring and summer (you'll need to book ahead to be sure of a place).

Brixton Windmill was built in 1816 and has been recently restored to its full glory. Children need to be big enough to climb a set of stairs to the first floor, and if they want to go further, taller than 1.2m. There are often events taking place outside the mill (we love their annual parade and festival every June, and they run five-a-side football tournaments, a harvest festival and Easter and Halloween events too), so there are things to do for the small ones who can't get inside, and tiny babies are happy enough to just stare at the sails.

Windmill Gardens, West end of Blenheim Gardens, Off Brixton Hill, SW2 5EU
brixtonwindmill.org
020 7926 6056
FREE
Open selected weekends through the spring and summer
⊖ **Brixton**

CELEBRATE SHAKESPEARE'S BIRTHDAY AT THE GLOBE THEATRE

Fairly difficult to miss, The Globe is a full-size reproduction of a 16th-century theatre perched proudly on the bank of the Thames.

Every year, on a Sunday near the 25 April they hold a proper, blow-out birthday bash for Shakespeare, with a day of free events. It's a great opportunity to go and have a look around this curious place. Kids will love the big day out; there are bands playing, jesters and entertainers, shows, classes, workshops and things to eat, plus, of course, actors declaiming and slapping their thighs in true Shakespearian fashion. Go and say happy bard-day to the dude with the beard and creative brain.

---

21 New Globe Walk, Bankside, SE1 9DT
shakespearesglobe.com
020 7401 9919
FREE 🍽 ♿ 🛒
See website for current opening times
⊖ **Blackfriars, Mansion House, London Bridge**

JOIN IN THE WORLD'S BIGGEST PILLOW FIGHT

The idea of International Pillow Fight Day is wonderfully simple. People hold pillow fights all over the world – from Atlanta to Zurich.

The official London event usually takes place in Trafalgar Square on a Saturday afternoon in March or April. There are only two rules: don't hit anyone with a camera and don't hit anyone without a pillow. Bring your own pillow (you can always use it to nap on the Tube on the way home).

It's enjoyable to watch for younger kids, and great fun to join in for older ones able to take a few (very gentle) knocks.

Trafalgar Square, WC2N 5DN
pillowfightday.com
FREE
See website for dates and times

⊖ **Leicester Square, Piccadilly Circus, Charing Cross, Embankment**

COOK EAST END PIE AND MASH

A real East End tradition; food doesn't get much more English than pie and mash, and this simplified version is easy to make yourself. This could be the centre of a St George's Day celebration dinner or even picnic if the weather is nice enough. For a full cockney feast, serve with jellied eels. Jelly! And eels! A wibbly-wobbly salty-fishy favourite of ours.

You'll need

For the filling
1 tbsp olive oil
1 onion, finely chopped
2 cloves of garlic, finely chopped
450g lean beef or steak mince
1 tsp English mustard
1 tbsp tomato purée
1 beef stock cube
vegetable oil
250ml beef stock
2 tbsp plain flour
salt and freshly ground black pepper

For the suet pastry
350g self-raising flour,
    plus extra for dusting
200g beef or vegetable suet
salt and freshly ground black pepper
large knob of butter, softened,
    for greasing

For the pie crust
450g ready-made shortcrust pastry
1 egg yolk, lightly beaten and mixed
    with a little milk

For the mash
2 large potatoes peeled, cut into chunks
100ml milk
knob of butter
salt and freshly grounded black pepper

For the parsley liquor
50g butter
50g cornflour
500ml chicken stock
generous bunch of curly parsley, finely
    chopped
½ clove of garlic, crushed with the back
    of a knife and a little sea salt

To serve
jellied eels (optional)

1. For the pie filling, heat the olive oil in a large frying pan over a medium heat and fry the onion for 10–15 minutes until fully softened. Add the garlic after 5 minutes. Add the mince and cook for 5 minutes, stirring occasionally, or until browned and cooked through. Stir in the rest of the filling ingredients and stir well, season with salt and freshly ground black pepper and set aside to cool.

2. Preheat the oven to 180°C/350°F/Gas 4.

3. For the suet pastry, sift the flour into a mixing bowl with the suet and season with salt and freshly ground black pepper. Gradually mix in about 4 tablespoons of cold water, or until you have a moist but firm dough. On a lightly floured surface, roll the dough out to a 2mm thickness.

4. Generously butter a largeish pie dish, then line with the suet pastry, so that it covers the base and sides completely. Spoon in the cooled filling mixture.

5. For the pie crust, roll out the ready-made shortcrust pastry on a lightly floured work surface to a 2mm thickness and use it to cover the pie, pushing down the edges firmly to seal all around. Brush generously with the beaten egg yolk and milk mixture. Make a hole in the middle of the pie lid to allow steam to escape.

6. Place the pie dish into a deep-sided roasting tin and pour in enough boiling water to come halfway up the side of the pie dish. Make sure not to get any water on the pastry. Transfer to the oven and cook for 20–30 minutes, or until the pastry is golden brown and the filling steaming hot.

7. Meanwhile, boil the potatoes for 20 minutes or until tender. Gently heat the milk in a pan, then mash the potatoes with the hot milk, butter and salt and freshly ground black pepper until smooth. Keep warm.

8. For the parsley liquor, melt the butter in a saucepan over a medium heat and stir in the cornflour to make a paste. Gradually stir in the chicken stock, bring to a simmer, then stir in the chopped parsley and crushed garlic and stir until thickened and smooth.

9. Serve out slices of hot pie with the mash, parsley liquor and jellied eels on the side, if you're brave!

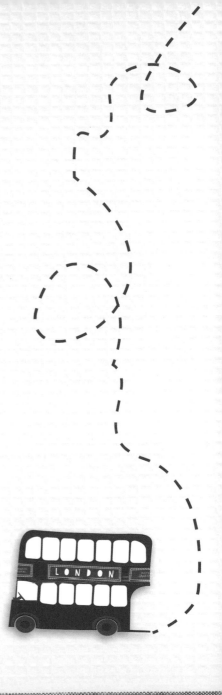

UNCOVER A TREAT
ON AN EASTER EGG HUNT

There is always a series of events across London (usually at family-friendly attractions) where kids can search for egg-shaped chocolatey treats. Kew Gardens (£££ kew.org) pulls out the big guns for its egg-stravaganza; past events have included an Inca chocolate trail, face-painting, an explorer train and chocolate-making classes.

In recent years, we've tracked down the fruits of the ship's chickens aboard the Cutty Sark (£££ page 86), searched for yolkers to the strains of baroque music at Handel House's (££ handelhouse.org) oh-so-elegant event and hunted for the artist-designed, giant eggs scattered around Covent Garden (FREE) – then snaffled some free Lindt goodies when we found them all! We've searched for chocolates in the grounds of the Geffrye Museum (FREE page 206) and decorated our own at Highgate's Lauderdale House (£ lauderdalehouse.co.uk).

Most National Trust properties in the capital run a series of egg hunts over the Easter holidays (££ page 64), with some properties waiving their entrance fees on certain days, and host special themed events such as fêtes and traditional egg-and-spoon races. Check their website for full details (nationaltrust.org.uk).

DISCOVER HIDDEN TREASURE IN THE MUSEUM OF LONDON*

Our city has been occupied since prehistoric times, so it's no surprise that buried treasures are constantly unearthed. The Museum of London hoards archaeological discoveries as well as more recent treasures (we once saw Tom Daley's swimming trunks in an exhibition!).

There's always something worth looking at in their temporary exhibition spaces (which can veer towards the gruesome on occasion), but their permanent exhibition space is more family-friendly. Play with a really fun model of the underground and overground system, try on a fire-fighter's helmet or go into a Saxon house. Every gallery in the museum has something for kids of all ages to really enjoy.

Activity-wise, during the week there are sweet play and sensory sessions for under-5s, but it's at weekends and holidays that things really start to get interesting for families. Their super-inventive digital workshops, history classes and craft sessions run by enthusiastic staff are on every weekend, as well as one-off events including May Day celebrations and Halloween spectaculars. The grump-filled Scrooge's Christmas Grotto has a special place in our hearts.

The museum walks a fine line between tourist attraction and community hub, and does it in style. The staff are friendly, eager to explain the exhibits, and understand what kids are interested in. We love this place.

- -

150 London Wall, EC2Y 5HN
museumoflondon.org.uk
020 7001 9844
FREE � ♿ 🛒
Open every day 10am–6pm
🚇 **Barbican, St Paul's**
The museum's indoor picnic spaces are open at weekends during term time and all week in the holidays, so pack a lunch.

- -

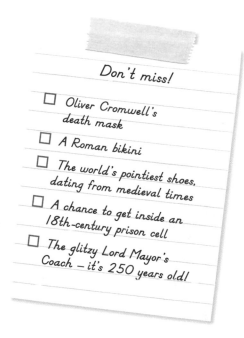

Don't miss!

- ☐ Oliver Cromwell's death mask
- ☐ A Roman bikini
- ☐ The world's pointiest shoes, dating from medieval times
- ☐ A chance to get inside an 18th-century prison cell
- ☐ The glitzy Lord Mayor's Coach – it's 250 years old!

BE INSPIRED BY CUTTING-EDGE INSTALLATIONS AT THE WHITECHAPEL GALLERY

Deep in the heart of East London, the Whitechapel Gallery is a hotbed of cutting-edge art and installations. Each year it hosts a Children's Art Commission show, where contemporary artists are invited to create kid-orientated work. Past participants have included Eva Rothschild, Simon and Tom Bloor and Jake and Dinos Chapman (and we have the colouring book to prove it). There are always some truly inspirational events to tie in with the exhibition each year.

The gallery is very, very family friendly; there are great baby-changing facilities and you can pick up an activity pack for kids from reception.

Family days are run throughout the year; expect activities that push kids' creative boundaries. There are also regular art and drawing courses and free arts festivals for teenagers.

After you've been around the exhibitions, head to the café for home-made Scotch eggs and bottles of posh pop.

77–82 Whitechapel High Street, E1 7QX
whitechapelgallery.org
020 7522 7888
FREE 🍵 ♿ 🚼
Open Tuesday–Sunday 11am–6pm, except Thursday 11am–9pm
🚇 Aldgate East, Aldgate, Whitechapel

GO SEE THE TARDIS AND PRETEND TO BE DOCTOR WHO

Got some mini-sci-fi buffs on your hands? Go and have your picture taken in front of a real-life TARDIS! Well, as real-life as TARDISes get. There's a real blue Police Box outside Earl's Court Tube that's great for posing for Doctor Who-and-assistant photographs. It was built in 1997 as a working box, but decommissioned in 2000. Take a bowtie or long scarf and pose, pose, pose.

Earl's Court Road, SW5 9QA
FREE
🚇 **Earl's Court**
Love Doctor Who? Why not visit the Who Shop in Upton Park, which is dedicated to all things Time Lord-related (thewhoshop.com) or, for hardcore fans, the Doctor Who walking tour, which takes in 15 locations from the TV show (£££ britmovietours.com).

BUST A MOVE AT EAST LONDON DANCE

If your lot are anything like ours, they're dance obsessed. TV talent shows and programmes such as *Glee* have made shimmying supercool and appealing to both boys and girls. If they want to brush up on their moves, or learn a new discipline, East London Dance runs free courses in a variety of styles; check out their On The Move streetdance classes (10+) and boys-only breakdance crew (11+). The classes take place in a network of community centres and theatres across the East of London.

eastlondondance.org
020 8279 1050
FREE
See website for dates, times and venues for classes

FLY A KITE ON STREATHAM COMMON

For one Sunday afternoon in April the skies above Lambeth are (breeze permitting) filled with all kinds of dancing, airborne displays for Streatham Common Kite Day. From huge stunt kites to music-accompanied performances, keep your eyes on the skies.

Kites are great things for kids to play with, but be sure to check in advance that your string is attached to the handle – we once came a cropper, as we got very excited when our kite flew higher and higher, only to realise too late that there was no knot on the end of the line. Bring your own kite, or browse the stalls and buy one, and join in with the fun. The Kite Day website even has some easy instructions on how to make a basic sled kite using a bin liner and some bamboo, so get creative and construct your own bespoke flyer.

Streatham High Road, SW16
streathamkiteday.org.uk
FREE &🚼
Open 11am–5pm
🚇 **Streatham, Streatham Common**

SPOT BLUEBELLS IN PERIVALE WOOD

There's nothing more exciting than exploring a part of London that no one usually sees – especially if that part of London is a dramatic, ancient oak forest. Perivale Wood is a nature reserve with a large chunk of fairytale wood, plus some scrubby bits, and pasture and streams and ponds. Once a year, on the last Sunday in April, its mysterious gates creak open and the public are allowed in – just like Wonka's factory, minus the chocolate and plus a whole load of twigs. It's at this time of year when the bluebells are most beautiful, so expect to see carpets of the nodding gentle flowers through the trees. Explore this sanctuary in the middle of the urban sprawl and pretend you've stepped into fairyland.

Under-16s can also join the junior wildlife group that meets at 1.45pm on the second Saturday of each month to pond-dip, hunt for mushrooms, bug-hunt and make bird boxes.

Off Sunley Gardens, Perivale, UB6 7PR
perivalewood.k-hosting.co.uk
FREE
Open the last Sunday in April, 10am–4.30pm
⊖ Perivale
Although there are a few stalls, facilities are limited, so come prepared with snacks or a picnic lunch.

APRIL

- [ ] Customise your own afikomen bag for Passover.

- [ ] Check to see if the Natural History Museum has opened its annual butterfly exhibition on the lawns outside the front of the building (nhm.ac.uk).

- [ ] Make windmills to brighten up your garden or balcony.

- [ ] Celebrate World Tapir Day (tapirday.org).

- [ ] Do some indoor gardening: grow cress or carrot tops on your windowsills.

- [ ] Make hot cross buns.

- [ ] Play some old-school April fool tricks; putting salt in a cup of tea and perching a bucket of water on top of a door are our favourites.

- [ ] Buy a bumper pack of googly eyes (eBay have big bags) and stick them on everything. Take pictures.

- [ ] Decorate your bike with streamers and ribbons ready for spring rides.

WEAR A JACK-IN-THE-GREEN COSTUME
FOR MAY DAY

The start of May is high season for folk dancers. Morrissers, hoodeners and maypole twirlers are all in demand across London to celebrate the start of fine weather and budding blossom. Every year, the headquarters of the English Folk Dance and Song Society, Cecil Sharp House in Camden, comes alive to the sound of stomping feet, jingling bells and lots of laughter, during their May in a Day festival. There's a ceilidh and maypole dancing, storytelling and singing, plus a chance to make a Jack-in-the-Green costume to wear in the grand parade at the end of the day. It's enormous fun, and very authentic, with more than a sniff of *The Wicker Man*.

You'll also find celebrations going on at other places across London. The V&A Museum of Childhood (pages 31, 65) usually dusts off its maypole and has a great knees-up. There are always fêtes taking place across the city, from traditional celebrations in leafy parks, to more hip gatherings in Shoreditch car parks.

Cecil Sharp House, 2 Regent's Park Road, NW1 7AY
efdss.org
020 7485 2206
££ ▣ ♿ ⛟

Open first Saturday in May 2pm–5pm
⎯ **Camden Town, Chalk Farm**
Be sure to visit the café in the basement of the venue
for truly delicious, home-made cakes.

COOK

MAY DAY HONEY CAKE

Make May Day even sweeter with this traditional Beltane Honey Cake. Eat it with a cup of tea to give you the energy to dance around the maypole.

You'll need

170g runny honey
140g butter, plus extra for greasing
85g light muscovado sugar
2 eggs, beaten
200g sifted self-raising flour

For the icing
55g sifted icing sugar
1 tbsp runny honey

1. Preheat the oven to 180°C/350°F/Gas 4, and butter and line the bottom of an 18cm round cake tin.

2. Put the honey, butter and muscovado sugar into a large pan. Add a tablespoon of water and heat slowly until melted.

3. Remove from the heat and mix in the eggs and flour until well combined.

4. Spoon the mixture into the cake tin and bake for 40–45 minutes until the cake is risen, springy to the touch and shrinking slightly from the sides of the tin.

5. Cool slightly in the tin before turning out onto a wire rack. While the cake is still warm, make the icing by mixing the icing sugar and honey together with 2–3 teaspoons of hot water. Drizzle over the cake, cool, then slice.

WALK ON WATER AT THE CANALWAY CAVALCADE*

Most kids don't often get to see the city's canals. Our hidden, green waterways are bursting with nature and have a vibrant community all of their own. The yearly Canalway Cavalcade, which takes place over the May Day Bank Holiday, celebrates boating life with a three-day festival at Little Venice. There's always tons going on for families, with events such as kayaking lessons, a chance to walk across the water in a giant plastic bubble, Punch and Judy shows and a Teddy Bear's Picnic. Check out the Puppet Theatre Barge (page 212) for tasters of their excellent shows.

Also expect Morris Dancers, boats to look at and explore and an illuminated procession of barges at 9pm on the Sunday night. Time to mess about on the river (or, strictly speaking, the canal).

Little Venice, Paddington, W2
waterways.org.uk
07979 676461
FREE 🚋 ♿ 🍴

Open Saturday 10am–6pm, Sunday 10am–6pm followed by music at 8.30pm and boat procession at 9.30pm, Monday 10am–5pm
🚇 Warwick Avenue, Edgware Road
Check website for best access routes; not all barges are wheelchair and buggy accessible.

LOOK OUT ACROSS THE CITY FROM THE MONUMENT*

Why pay big bucks to go on the London Eye or ascend The Shard when for only a few pounds and a bit of a puff you can see a pigeon's-eye view of the city?

Standing 62m tall and designed by Sir Christopher Wren, The Monument marks the place where the Great Fire of London started in 1671. It's a fabulous place to climb up, take in the panorama and view the ever-changing cityscape through one of the column's talking telescopes, although nervous kids (and adults) may find it a challenge to step out onto the viewing platform. Make sure to take your certificate of ascent on your way out. Those without a head for heights (or with an unwieldy buggy) can take a look at live images from the top of the tower on a viewing screen at the bottom.

Buy an affordable joint ticket with Tower Bridge (towerbridge.org.uk) for a tip-top day out.

Fish Street Hill, EC3R 6DB
themonument.info
020 7626 2717
£

**Open April–September 9.30am–6pm (last entry 5:30pm);
October–March 9.30am–5.30pm (last entry 5pm)**
🚇 Monument

Did you know?

The Monument is also a scientific instrument. Its central shaft was designed to be used as a zenith telescope (although wind and vibrations scuppered this), but it has been used for pendulum experiments. Each step up to the platform is six inches high, so the whole building can been used for barometric pressure studies. There's even a secret laboratory under the building (take a peek through a grate in the floor to see it).

SLIDE DOWN THE HELTER-SKELTER AT CHESTNUT SUNDAY

Celebrate the chestnut blossom in Bushy Park in a truly old-fashioned way. Every year, on the Sunday closest to 11 May, locals put on a fair for Chestnut Sunday. The fun starts with a parade through the park, followed by some classic retro-tainment. Take in historical reenactments, vintage carousels and helter-skelters (be ready with your camera for super-cute pictures), loads of classic cars, pony rides and live music. Hope for loads of sunshine, bring a picnic and party like it's 1959.

Bushy Park, TW11 0EQ
fbhp.org.uk
020 8979 1586
FREE ☕ ♿ ✄
Open 12.30pm–4.30pm (timings can vary, so check the website)
🚇 Teddington, Hampton Wick, Hampton Court

SHOUT 'HE'S BEHIND YOU' AT THE PUPPET FESTIVAL

Some kids delight in them, while others scream in terror; find out which camp your nippers are in at the annual Covent Garden Puppet Festival on the second Sunday in May. Centred around St Paul's Church, there are stacks of puppet booths competing for your attention, brass bands and a church service conducted by Mr Punch (which is, frankly, terrifying). There's also live music, puppet workshops and May Fair delights including maypole dancing, juggling and clowns.

St Paul's Church Garden, Bedford Street, WC2E 9ED
020 7836 5221
FREE ☕ ♿ ✄
Open second Sunday in May 11am–5.30pm
🚇 Covent Garden, Leicester Square, Embankment
There are loads of great family-friendly places to eat in Covent Garden. Our lot love popping the edamame beans from their shells at Wagamama, or you can go for chips and mussels at Belgos.

MAKE LIKE A PIRATE ON THE CUTTY SARK

Shiver me timbers and splice the mainbrace! Every May the Cutty Sark is over-run with pocket-sized pirates. The 19th-century tea clipper is always a fantastic place to visit, but for one Sunday every year, she's even more fun. She's made a spectacular recovery from the fire in 2007 that almost destroyed her, and you can now walk underneath her as well as across her decks.

Buccaneer costumes are mandatory for the Pirate Party (there's a competition), and events include storytelling, bandana and telescope making, exciting displays of original pirate documents (who knows, maybe even a real treasure map!) and a plunderers' treasure trail to follow. It is a little on the expensive side to get on board the ship, but if you're going to go, this is the day to do it. You can even have a cup of tea and slice of scrumptious cake in the Even Keel Café beneath her bows. Make sure you set aside time for a trip up to the top of the hill in Greenwich Park, and perhaps a quick sail around the (FREE) Maritime Museum (page 52).

King William Walk, Greenwich, SE10 9HT
rmg.co.uk/cuttysark/
020 8858 4422
£££ 🍺 ♿ 🚲
Open 10am–5pm (last entry 4pm)
🚇 Cutty Sark
Wheelchair access limited to three at any one time. Buggies can be parked outside the entrance (we always have a bike lock strapped to ours for just such occasions). Pre-book your ticket and jump the queue.

DIG UP HISTORY AT NUNHEAD CEMETERY

Holy skulls! Nunhead Cemetery in South London is a 52-acre, rambling, overgrown Victorian burial ground, rammed with gothic graves covered in ivy, weeping angels (try not to think about that *Doctor Who* episode) and marvellous inscriptions to uncover.

Every May, on a Sunday, they hold their once-a-year open day, which means the secret crypt (*secret crypt!*) is unlocked for special tours and the ruined chapel is opened up. There are also stalls and kid-friendly activities such as bug-hunting, face-painting and craft sessions, plus, of course, the magnificent cemetery to explore.

Linden Grove, SE15 3LP
fonc.org.uk
FREE   ♿ 🚼
Open every day 11am–5pm
🚇 **Nunhead, Peckham Rye**

BUILD YOUR OWN SCULPTURE AT TATE BRITAIN

Tate Britain might not have the blockbuster appeal of its brasher, younger sibling, Tate Modern, but it's less crowded and much quieter.

A truly great place to spend the day with your gang. Your little Barbara Hepworths can even make their own contribution to a real work of art. *Liminal*, created by artists Abigail Hunt and Kieren Reed, is a series of wooden blocks that is sturdy enough to stand on and chuck around, and which acts as an ever-changing sculpture, formed and shaped by visitors to the gallery (mainly kids). The sculpture can even be used in other ways; for example, the gallery has used it as seating for a series of film screenings. It's a simple but really lovely idea, and very empowering for little artists.

Millbank, SW1P 4RG
tate.org.uk
020 7887 8888
FREE 💷 ♿ 🚼
Open every day 10am–6pm. *Liminal:* **every weekend and Thursdays and Fridays in the school holidays, 11am–3pm**
🚇 **Pimlico, Vauxhall, Westminster**

ASK A BOFFIN ANY QUESTION YOU LIKE AT THE IMPERIAL FESTIVAL

Do your nippers ask a lot of questions? Of course they do, they're kids. A trip to May's Imperial Festival might, however, give you a break for a few hours.

Held at Imperial College, home to some of the finest boffins in the land, this celebration of science, culture, creativity and general craziness will get your kids inspired about the world around them. Every child will have a zillion things to ask about the science demos, talks and events happening around the college, and luckily there are friendly, brainy folk on hand who are more than happy to answer them.

This enormous festival is rammed with loads of things to do; past events have included finding a strawberry's DNA, firing a toy air gun to simulate battle injuries, dance classes, displays of old cars and cars of the future, a skateboarding Isaac Newton and a mechanical dragon. And that's not even scratching the surface. There is also music, displays and a pub for parents to cower in (called the Haemo Globe Inn).

It's an unabashed nerdfest, and even more fun than an explosion in a chemistry lab (expect some of those too).

South Kensington Campus, Exhibition Road, SW7 2AZ
imperial.ac.uk/festival
020 7594 8198
FREE ☕ ♿ 🍼
Open Friday–Saturday in early May. See website for details
🚇 **South Kensington**

SLEEP OVER AT THE MUSEUM

Every year, galleries and exhibition venues across London keep their doors open way past their usual closing time for the annual Museums at Night celebrations. Many of the events are adults-only, but there are a few, very special happenings for which it's well worth staying up past bedtime.

Events include sleepovers, film screenings and dancing. Most of the more kid-friendly stuff takes place in the early evening; keep an eye on the National Maritime Museum and the Royal Observatory's website (page 52) to see what they have up their sleeves, as well as the Royal Palaces (hrp.org.uk) and the National Army Museum (nam.ac.uk).

MONA LISA

PICASSO

VAN GOGH

KAHLO

Across London
culture24.org.uk/places-to-go/museums-at-night/
01273 623 266
FREE–£££
**Held the weekend nearest May 18 (International Museums Day),
Thursday–Saturday**

WANDER

As well as the high-concept art installations and slightly impenetrable performances, there are always stacks of family-friendly events going on at this annual, three-week event.

THROUGH

Most family friendly of all is the yearly *Shimmy*, held in St Mary's Church Square and the environs, which is a collision of kid-enchanting, site-specific arts pieces from the likes of Battersea Arts Centre and Emergency Exit

ARTWORKS

Arts, plus free workshops and fun activities. It's all a bit mysterious, with specific events kept a bit of a secret until the actual day, but previous years have involved a huge conga, a community-made kilometre of silk bunting, junk sculptures, a bicycle ballet and spectacular performance and dance pieces.

St Mary's Church Square, Putney High Street, Putney SW15 1SN
wandsworthartsfestival.com
020 8871 8711
FREE ♿ 🚼
Open every day 1pm–5pm. See website for dates and venues
🚇 Putney Bridge, East Putney

AT THE WANDSWORTH ARTS FESTIVAL

GO BRASS RUBBING
AT ST MARTIN-IN-THE-FIELDS

Perfect for a rainy May day, a brass-rubbing session at St Martin-in-the-Fields is creative, fairly cheap and teaches kids about history. Rubbing is easy; you tape some paper over a brass memorial plaque, then rub coloured wax across the paper in order to capture the textures and patterns in the brass.

Staff are on hand to provide guidance and materials, including specialist papers and metallic waxes, and visitors can choose from brasses depicting knights, dragons, elegant ladies in costume and other images that can't fail to appeal to young children.

The church is dead central, so it's a brilliant place to meet up with friends or to combine with a trip to the National Gallery (page 12), or the National Portrait Gallery (npg.org.uk).

Trafalgar Square, WC2N 4JJ
stmartin-in-the-fields.org
020 7766 1100
£ 🍽 ♿ 🚹
Open Monday–Wednesday 10am–6pm, Thursday–Saturday 10am–8pm, Sunday 11.30am–5pm. Check website for opening hours of church outside of brass-rubbing times
⊖ **Charing Cross, Leicester Square**

TOP TIP
The excellent Café in the Crypt in the basement of the church is a great step-off point to refuel on home-made cakes and soup, and chill out in the centre of town. There's something about its architecture that seems to absorb sound (which, if you've got noisy kids, can only be a good thing).

GO FOSSIL-HUNTING AT THE GRANT MUSEUM OF ZOOLOGY

The Grant Museum of Zoology is a great place for kids who are into weirder, ickier, animal-related stuff to spend an afternoon. Its collections of skeletons, pickled beasts, brains in embalming fluid, long-extinct animals and bisected heads hold a gruesome appeal for children. Check out the gigantic snake skeleton, dodo bones and jar of moles. One of the venue's rooms has been converted into a *Micrarium* – a back-lit display of the museum's collection of weeny, interesting creatures where you can peer at slides containing specimens of tiny winged creatures, micro-sea dwellers and titchy spiders.

The museum is small, which means it really makes an effort; their temporary exhibitions are fascinating (we loved, loved, loved the display of animal-created art) and their kids' events are inventive. They have a lot of handle-the-exhibits events, and they sometimes get out a big tank through which kids can sift to find fossils to take home.

Rockefeller Building, UCL, 21 University Street, WC1E 6DE
ucl.ac.uk/museums/zoology
020 3108 2052
FREE ♨ ⚬ ⚲
Open Monday–Saturday 1pm–5pm
⊖ Warren Street, Euston Square
There's an eat-in branch of Planet Organic on Torrington Place near the museum. Nip in there afterwards for really good coffee and smoothies and a cram-all-you-can-into-a-container, super-healthy, good-value lunch.

WRITE A POEM AT THE LONDON LITERATURE FESTIVAL

This annual celebration of words takes place at the Southbank Centre. Of course, there's a lot going on for adults, but it's the jaw-dropping range of kids' events at this festival that we adore.

The Southbank Centre does multi-faceted, large-scale festivals really well, and, of course, it's mainly under cover, so weather isn't an issue. Their kids' programme includes free poetry jams and games in the gigantic Clore Ballroom, children's author events, signings and workshops, and other truly inventive happenings. We loved 2013's Superhero Run, where poet Charlie Dark took a bunch of masked kids on a dash around the building, with little pop-up performances happening around every corner, and the Spin session that pitched poets against rappers in a blistering, silly war of words.

The festival is a gentle way to get your kids thinking about the power of stories, and their events help make words leap off the page and become a powerful tool for children.

Southbank Centre, Belvedere Road, SE1 8XX
southbankcentre.co.uk/whatson/festivals-series/london-literature-festival
020 7960 4200
FREE–£££ 🎦 ♿ ✗
Open 10am–11pm
🚇 **Waterloo, Embankment, Charing Cross**

BECOME A MUDLARK AT THE MUSEUM OF LONDON DOCKLANDS*

Although it's only been around for just over ten years, the Museum of London Docklands is one of our very favourite places to take our brood, and the compact-but-awesome East London museum's free weekly kids' events are already an institution.

Housed in a 19th-century warehouse, the museum concentrates on the intensely rich history of the city's East End, telling stories of the area's trade links, the colourful history of the port, the assault the area suffered in the Second World War and its current role as a glittering, shiny financial centre. Kids will love the iron gibbet that was used to hang bodies of pirates over the Thames and the life-sized reconstruction of some (slightly scary and a bit smelly) Victorian streets. It's worth going for the brilliant, under-12 kids' soft-play area, Mudlarks, alone, while in the children gallery there's also cargo you can weigh, a tea clipper to load and a diver's helmet to try on.

The museum also provides a really varied and fun menu of family activities at weekends and during the holidays. In the past, they've held May Day celebrations (building a Jack-in-the-Green figure) and a Chinese New Year party, taught Victorian street games and created giant artworks along the quayside. It's a lovely, welcoming place that feels like a real part of the local community.

West India Quay, Canary Wharf, E14 4AL
museumoflondon.org.uk/docklands/
020 7001 9844
FREE ☕ ♿ ⚲
Open Monday–Sunday 10am–6pm
⊖ Canary Wharf, West India Quay
The museum's Rum & Sugar restaurant is lovely, but a little pricey. Pop into the café on the ground floor for good-value snacks.

MAY

- [ ] Use the Open Space finder (www.gigl.org.uk/) to locate your nearest open-access patch of land (you may be surprised at what you turn up).

- [ ] Celebrate Vaisakhi in Trafalgar Square (london.gov.uk/get-involved/events).

- [ ] Buy a pair of plain pumps for the summer and customise them using fabric pens.

- [ ] Rub shoulders with real-life famous painters at the Art Car Boot Fair (artcarbootfair.com).

- [ ] Take in some street art at the Dulwich Festival (dulwichfestival.co.uk).

- [ ] Check out the line-up for this year's Udderbelly festival on the South Bank — their kids' shows are superb! (underbelly.co.uk/udderbelly-festival-at-southbank-centre).

- [ ] Get in free to Ham House on their community day (nationaltrust.org.uk).

- [ ] Ogle beautiful old vehicles at the Enfield Pageant of Motoring (whitewebbsmuseum.co.uk/html/body_enfield_pageant.html).

- [ ] Head east to Dalston for the magical Land of Kids festival (landofkids.co.uk).

MAKE MAGNIFICENT ART AT SOMERSET HOUSE*

We adore going to Somerset House. It's a brilliant place for nippers to cut loose and have a good run around while their parents hang out and drink a well-made coffee from one of the many excellent places to eat in the building.

What we love most about the place, however, are the untoppable and fiercely creative art workshops. Every month, the venue hosts one of the best free classes for kids in London, themed around an exhibition. They're great for kids aged 6–12 and their families; past events have included making a gigantic mechanical puppet with set designer Andy Hillman, creating eye-popping collages inspired by Cartier-Bresson and animal print designs similar to those in the venue's Valentino fashion exhibition. It's a properly inspiring, hip place for families to hang out, rain or shine.

Strand, WC2R 1LA
somersethouse.org.uk
020 7845 4600
FREE–££ 🍽 ♿ 🛒

Open every day 10am–11pm. Term-time workshops run on one Saturday in the month, 11am–3pm, on a drop-in basis. There are more workshops through school holidays; check website for details.
🚇 Temple, Covent Garden, Charing Cross, Embankment
*The Courtauld Gallery (home to some of the biggest exhibitions at the venue) is **FREE** for under-18s.*

Don't forget!

If it's sunny, be sure to stash your swimming costumes and a towel in your bag. Kids and water are a great combination, and they will absolutely love running through (and sitting on top of) the choreographed fountains that erupt across the courtyard (see page 137).

There are some places in London we've always wanted to explore. So many leafy spaces in the capital are fenced off, and some gardens can only be glimpsed through locked gates. But for one weekend in June each year those gates are unlocked in a celebration of communal spaces.

Highlights have included getting to see (and perhaps walk on) the sharp, formal lawns of Eaton Square, admiring Cable Street's community garden, taking a tour of the medicinal plants of the Royal College of Physicians garden, discovering unexpected allotments slap-bang in the middle of Regent's Park and visiting the flamboyant Roof Gardens in Kensington (home to four flamingos).

Some very special places have tickets allocated by ballot only, so you'll need to get your shout in early to gain access to the back yard of 10 Downing Street. Many of the gardens run child-friendly events such as Punch and Judy shows, art sessions, sports activities and gardening classes.

Venues across London
opensquares.org
££ Under-12s go FREE
Open second Saturday–Sunday in June, 11am–5pm
Many gardens are wheelchair/buggy friendly, but check on the website ahead of your visit.

PHYSICIANS AND FLAMINGOS AT THE OPEN SQUARES WEEKEND

MAKE A PUPPET
WITH THE LITTLE ANGEL THEATRE

The Little Angel Theatre in Islington has been the 'home of British puppetry' for over 50 years. With a strong bias towards children's theatre, its figurine-based productions are always inventive and magical, incorporating video and avant-garde techniques as well as more traditional marionettes, shadow-play and glove-puppets. They are often the first to premiere shows that go on to tour other theatres, and we're fans of their festivals of brand-new, cutting-edge work and puppet-related films. For more serious enthusiasts, there are also regular workshops, courses and discussion groups.

They hold a free summer party every June with stalls and games, which is a lot of fun and allows visitors a peep behind the scenes, plus a chance to meet the puppeteers as well as create their own puppet.

14 Dagmar Passage, N1 2DN
littleangeltheatre.com
020 7226 1787
FREE–£££ 🍴 ♿ 🚼
Party held one Saturday in June or early July. See website for other events and productions
🚇 **Angel, Highbury and Islington**
All year round the theatre holds baby-friendly and 'relaxed' performances tailored to audiences of children and adults with special needs.

MEET YOUR NEIGHBOURS AT THE BIG LUNCH

The accepted wisdom is that Londoners don't want to get to know their neighbours. We say 'Pah!' to that.

The Big Lunch is a yearly event that was devised by the Eden Project in 2009 and aims to bring communities together for a sociable gathering – with delicious food! Win, win, win. This is an event in which children can really get involved; they can make decorations, help design menus, make simple dishes and act as hosts (there's nothing cuter than a kid pretending to be a waiter). There are always a load of ready-set-up lunches across the city to join, or start your own!

thebiglunch.com
FREE
Held on the first Sunday in June, on YOUR street
Download posters and information from the website.

COOK

PICNIC LOAF

This delicious savoury loaf is big enough for 4–6 people to share as part of the Big Lunch. It's really transportable, so it won't fall apart as you take it to your party.

You'll need

- 2 red peppers, halved and deseeded
- 1 medium courgette, thinly sliced
- 2 tbsp olive oil
- 20g sun-dried tomatoes, chopped
- 20 fresh basil leaves
- 800g unsliced white bloomer loaf
- 100g extra-mature Cheddar, grated
- 50g thinly sliced salami
- 70g rocket leaves
- 125g thinly sliced ham
- 125g sliced mozzarella

1. Preheat the oven to 200°C/400°F/Gas 6. Cut the pepper halves into 4 and place in a roasting tin with the sliced courgette. Drizzle over the olive oil, season with black pepper and toss together. Roast for 15–20 minutes until softened and golden. Remove from the oven and stir in the sun-dried tomatoes and basil leaves, then set aside to cool.

2. With a serrated knife, horizontally slice the very top off the loaf and set aside. Scoop out the bread from the middle of the loaf, leaving a 2cm edge all the way round. (Keep the scooped-out bread for making breadcrumbs.) Spoon one-third of the roasted vegetables mix into the base of the loaf, pressing them in firmly.

3. Top with the grated Cheddar and then the salami slices. Top with half the rocket leaves, pressing down well. Add another third of the roasted vegetables followed by the ham slices and then the sliced mozzarella. Top with the remaining rocket and roasted vegetables and press down firmly. Place the top back on the loaf, tightly wrap, first in cling film and then in foil, ready to transport. Chill in the fridge.

4. Once at the picnic, cut into slices to serve.

STYLE IT OUT AT THE MARYLEBONE FAYRE

The Marylebone Fayre might look like a cosy, market-town fête, but scratch below the surface and the benefits of its central location are apparent. It's *very* fashion. The coconut shy is run by Cath Kidston, there's a bike-powered smoothie maker and the music stage is populated by some of the capital's brightest upcoming talents.

There are loads of kid-specific activities: you can make juggling balls, climb Spider Mountain, try the bungee trampoline or ride a Victorian carousel. Be sure to get there hungry, as food stalls sell modish grub such as mac 'n' cheese, churros and posh ice lollies supplied by top foodie joints such as Byron and The Real Greek. Yum.

Marylebone High Street, W1U 5HD
marylebonesummerfayre.com
FREE ⬛ ♿ 👶
Open third Sunday in June, 10am–5pm
🚇 Baker Street, Regent's Park

GET THE LOWDOWN ON BRIT ART AT THE SOUTH LONDON GALLERY

The South London Gallery in Peckham is renowned for its cutting-edge curation and thought-provoking work on display. They get kids involved in their temporary exhibitions through creative and fun Sunday Spot kids workshops. In a free session that is perfect for 3–12-year-olds, an artist leads the group, explaining and exploring the work that is currently on display at the graceful venue, They also run off-site art and play sessions at estates close to the gallery. Don't miss lunch at their excellent café, No67. A warning: we had a coconut latte there and two months later were still getting pangs for another.

65–67 Peckham Road, SE5 8UH
southlondongallery.org
020 7703 6120
FREE ⬛ ♿ 👶
Open Tuesday–Sunday 11am–6pm,
except Wednesday 11am–9pm
🚇 Denmark Hill

GET A TASTE OF THE TRADITIONAL AT TROOPING THE COLOUR

Sometimes it's great to wallow in traditional London; the bits that tourists get excited about. It feels almost like going on holiday in your own city. Trooping the Colour, has been taking place in June since 1748, when bands and a massed parade of soldiers are inspected by the Queen and an RAF fly-past roars overhead to mark the monarch's official birthday. It's all very formal, but it's a real connection with history.

You can stand in the Mall or St James's Park early to bag a good view but, sadly, unless you applied in January, the allocated tickets will have gone months ago. If you don't get a good spot, the fly-past should be visible from most of central London.

Horse Guards Parade, Whitehall, SW1A 2AX
royal.gov.uk/royaleventsandceremonies/troopingthecolour/troopingthecolour.aspx
FREE 🍵 ♿ 👶
Open one Saturday in June 10am, flypast at 1pm
⊖ **Charing Cross, Westminster**

TOP TIP

One week and two weeks before the parade there are two full dress rehearsals, known as the Major General's Review and Colonel's Review. Watch either for all of the spectacle, minus the crowds (and, er, the Queen).

ALL ABOARD BROCKWELL PARK'S TINY TRAIN

Our little train lovers clamour to ride the tiny engine that runs through Brockwell Park on Sundays between March and October. It's only £1 for a return (free for under-2s), which will take you all the way from the Herne Hill gates to the Brockwell Lido (great for a splash in warm weather). It's dead cute, really traditional and adults adore it too.

Afterwards, treat yourselves to breakfast pancakes at the absolutely cracking Brockwell Lido Café.

Dulwich Road, SE24 0PA
travelbpmr.com/
07973 613515
£
Open Sundays, March–October, 11am–4pm
(weather dependant)
⏺ Herne Hill

GET A CUTE OVERLOAD AT PUP IDOL

We adore dog shows, and the annual Pup Idol event, which takes place at the Spaniards Inn in Hampstead (one of Hopscotch's favourite family dining stop-offs) gets our Best In Show Award.

Do your best to avoid the pleading eyes of the dogs needing homes and focus on the main events. The categories are fantastic: Best-Dressed Dog, Owner/Dog Lookalike and Golden Oldie are all favourites, and kids will yap with delight at the Cutest Pup competition. They reckon it's 'London's coolest dog show' and they're not far off – Liam Gallagher (cool-ish) is a regular and Bill Oddie (supercool!) has judged in the past.

Spaniards Road, Hampstead, NW3 7JJ
alldogsmatter.co.uk/
020 8341 3196
FREE (££ to enter your dog in the competition) 🚇 ♿ 🚼
Open 10.30am–3pm
⏺ Golders Green

EXPLORE THE BOOKSHOPS WITH YOUR BOOKWORMS AT THE CHARING CROSS ROAD FESTIVAL

Charing Cross Road is best known for its huge numbers of bookshops, so it's extremely appropriate that its yearly festival has a heavy literary theme. There are readings by kids' authors, signings, crafts themed around books and treasure trails to follow. Plus there are free food giveaways, live music and special book sales. All events are housed in shops and cafés along the road (and neighbouring Denmark Street or Tin Pan Alley), so it doesn't matter if it rains (yes, it's June, but this is Britain.)

lovecharingcrossroad.com

Foyles
113–119 Charing Cross Road, WC2H 0EB
020 7434 1574
FREE ♿ 🚼
Open Saturday 9.30am–9pm (festival events from 11am–6pm),
Sunday 11.30am–6pm (festival events from 2pm)
🚇 **Leicester Square, Tottenham Court Road**

Blackwells
100 Charing Cross Road, WC2H 0JG
020 7292 5100
FREE ♿ 🚼
Open Saturday 9.30am–8pm (festival events from 11am–6pm),
Sunday 12pm–6pm (festival events from 2pm)
🚇 **Leicester Square, Tottenham Court Road**

CATCH A CRAB
IN DEPTFORD CREEK*

London probably isn't the first place you'd think of going crabbing, but the brackish waters of Deptford Creek are home to millions of the clawed crustacea, as well as eels, flounders and shrimps.

The Creekside Education Trust run days themed around den building and cooking over an open fire, bug-hunting, mudlarking, making recycled art sculptures and crab fishing. All activities we'd love our London kids to get a taste of. Just bring your wellies; all other equipment is supplied. Age ranges for courses range from 3+ to 8+ and kids can be left in the care of the centre (£).

Adults and older kids will also love Creekside's monthly low-tide walks (£££) for a duck's-eye view of the rapidly changing banks' history and wildlife. It's an utterly unique trip, and a weirdly moving experience you'll remember for a long time. Kids must be over 8 and accompanied by an adult.

14 Creekside, Deptford, SE8 4SA
creeksidecentre.org.uk
020 8692 9922
FREE–£££ ♿ 🚼
See website for dates and times
⊖ **Greenwich, Deptford, Deptford Bridge**
Wheelchair users can't get down into the creek, but the centre has a new accessible pond and is dedicated to making as many as possible of its activities accessible for mobility-impaired people.

TAP DANCE TO TRAFALGAR SQUARE TO SEE THE BEST OF THE WEST END SHOWS FOR FREE

Travelling through London, the big musicals are constantly in your face. There are ads in Tube stations, lighted signs above the theatres and snaking queues of tourists patiently waiting outside their doors, but taking in a show is a pricey proposition, especially for families. This is why we head down to Trafalgar Square for their annual *West End Live* show and get a free taster of some of the very best musicals, shows and plays in town. The casts of some of the top current shows in London bring their golden voices and diamond toes to the outdoor stage; the show includes excerpts from long-running musicals, kid-friendly shows and the biggest names in the business.

Who knows, maybe one of our kids might be inspired to take to the West End stage (*actually* our dream). Get there early to make sure you get in, and, if you can, avoid taking a buggy.

Trafalgar Square, WC2N 5DN
westendlive.co.uk
020 7641 3297
FREE &♿ 🛒
Open Saturday 11am–6pm, Sunday 12pm–6pm
🚇 **Leicester Square, Piccadilly Circus, Charing Cross, Embankment**

CRAFTS AND COCONUTS AT GREEN DAYS

The Green Days festival is, deep down, an old-fashioned summer fête; timeless, reassuring and wholesome fun. The all-weekender first took place in 1967 with Poet Laureate John Betjeman as its patron in a bid to raise awareness of the threat to local Victorian architecture by developers. The event now raises much-needed money for local restoration projects and charities.

There's a special area for kids with art workshops, games and mini-stalls, but there's lots going on for the adults too. Flex your winning arm at the coconut shy, hang out at the bandstand and browse the craft fair, or get your costumes out for the fancy dress competition, watch the five-a-side football contest and even get some free basic repairs done on the family bikes.

Acton Green Common, W4 1LR
bedfordparkfestival.org
020 8994 1380
FREE 🚆 ♿ 🚼
Open second weekend in June
⊖ Turnham Green

GO ON A SCAVENGER HUNT

Scavenger hunts are awesome fun for both kids and adults. Kids get to spend time outside in the sun, bombing around with their mates and having a blast, while adults get half-an-hour's peace. Head for your nearest park or woodland (find your nearest open spaces at gigl.org.uk and see if you can find:

- ☐ Pine cones
- ☐ Feathers
- ☐ A really pretty stone
- ☐ A four-leaf clover
- ☐ Something shiny
- ☐ Something red
- ☐ A stick that looks like something else
- ☐ A leaf with pointy edges
- ☐ Something round
- ☐ A seed
- ☐ A lolly stick

When Carters Fair pulls into the park nearest us, it makes our hearts soar. A lovingly restored collection of steam-powered, vintage Victorian rides, sideshows, stalls and games, the red-and-yellow painted wagons signal that there's a great afternoon in store for us all. The fair first opened in Battersea Park in 1980 and is now a London summer institution.

We like to take a picnic and make a day of it. There are golden galloping horses to ride, tiny trains to board, dodgems to squeal on and helter-skelters to slide down. The gleaming retro colours are like a Cath Kidston print come to life, and are a brilliant background for cute, Instagram-friendly snaps of kids.

Our favourite sideshow is the Wall of Death, where vintage motorbikes roar around a huge drum, coming ever closer to the crowd peering over the top.

The fair is free to enter, so go in and take your time wandering round. Ride costs can mount up, so check online for money-off vouchers and bargain tickets ahead of time.

All summer, in parks across London
carterssteamfair.co.uk
01628 826693
Location Information Line: 01628 822221
FREE–£££ ☕ ♿ 🚼
Open 12pm–late

TOP TIP

The fair also often has a firework display on Saturday nights, which is an added, free bonus.

For small tinkers into battles and war, this is really thrilling. Every weekend between the end of March and the end of August, the Battle of Britain Bunker at RAF Uxbridge is open to the public. It's 18m below ground (accessed by steps), and has tons of untouched army hardware to gawk at, including a plotting room with one of those really cool gigantic tables that mark the situations of enemy planes and troops.

There's no need to book at weekends. Visiting the bunker feels truly exciting; it's not a 'museum experience', it's the real thing, in all its unpolished, raw glory. It's enthralling for older kids, and a direct link to our recent history that brings to life what they learn at school. There's a 76-step staircase leading down into the bunker, so wear flat shoes.

St Andrew's Road, UB10 0RN
raf.mod.uk/battleofbritainbunker
01895 238154
FREE suggested donation £
Open summer weekends 10am–4pm
Uxbridge

GO DEEP UNDERGROUND AT THE RAF BUNKER

MAKE A GIANT ROBOT AT CAMDEN ARTS CENTRE

The biggest arts centre in North London, Camden Arts Centre showcases work from cutting-edge modern artists and makes it totally accessible to kids.

Each exhibition is accompanied by a series of free Sunday workshops where children enjoy games and create pieces of art that reflect the work on show in the gallery.

We've enjoyed making giant robots inspired by the art of Bruce Lacey, have been inspired by prehistoric vegetation to make ceramic plants from press moulds and created stunning time-lapse films in the garden.

The venue makes great use of its beautiful grounds and kids often get creative with natural materials. Be sure to grab lunch in the centre's great café – their noodles are out of this world.

Arkwright Road, NW3 6DG
camdenartscentre.org
020 7472 5500
FREE
Open Tuesday–Sunday 10am–6pm;
Wednesday 10am–9pm; Workshops Sunday 2pm
Finchley Road and Frognal

MEET BRITAIN'S FINEST IN KENSAL GREEN CEMETERY

Junior Wednesday and Pugsley Addamses will nod gravely in delight at the thought of Kensal Green Cemetery's open day. The most fashionable of London's cemeteries in the 19th century, here you will find the final resting places of hundreds of the most famous names in history. In June this West London necropolis swings open its gates for as fun-filled a day as it's possible to have surrounded by dead people. Expect attractions such as a parade of vintage hearses, stalls and great people-watching opportunities.

Get there early to book a place on one of the popular tours (£). The trip around the catacombs is fascinating, and a little scary, but bear in mind that children under the age of 12 aren't permitted into the shadowy holes under the church. However, there are plenty of other walks they can participate in, and exploring the cemetery unguided is huge fun.

Harrow Road, W10 4RA
kensalgreen.co.uk
020 8969 0152
FREE 🚇 👶
Open 11am–5pm
🚇 **Kensal Green, Willesden Junction, Ladbroke Grove**
Wheelchair and buggy access to the chapels and buildings is poor.
The cemetery is open to visitors the rest of year, and tours are
available some Sundays. Check the website for details.

Spot the grave!
Which of these famous people from history's tombs will you spot?

☐ Tightrope walker Emile Blondin

☐ Engineer Isambard Kingdom Brunel

☐ Writer William Makepeace Thackeray

☐ Victorian novelist Wilkie Collins

☐ Mathematician and inventor Charles Babbage

☐ Playwright Harold Pinter

CELEBRATE YOUR COMMUNITY AT LONDON PRIDE

Pride, the yearly celebration of all things gay, lesbian, transgender and anything in between takes place on the Saturday nearest the anniversary of the Stonewall riots (28 June).

The main parade through the centre of London (the route changes year to year) is great fun, with roller derby teams, bands, dance groups and, of course, some truly outrageous costumes. It might be a bit full-on for smaller kids, but Pride organisers are at pains to stress the family-friendly nature of the event. There is always provision for kids, but, as the event has had a rocky financial history, that provision can vary from a 'kids' area' in a small square in Soho, to a full mini-festival picnic for families in a park in Vauxhall.

Keep your eye on listings to find out what's going on this year.

londoncommunitypride.org
FREE &♿ 🚼
Parade takes place the Saturday nearest 28 June

JUNE

☐ *Book ahead for Kids Week (under-16s go free to West End shows in August) — see kidsweek.co.uk.*

☐ *Celebrate Father's Day with a trip to the National Army Museum in Chelsea (nam.ac.uk); they usually have a special event for the occasion.*

☐ *Learn how to make lemonade.*

☐ *Try juggling on World Juggling Day.*

☐ *Watch Wimbledon on one of the big screens that pop up around town.*

☐ *Use up all those unplanted seeds (we always seem to have some left over) to make collages.*

☐ *Take a trip to the South Bank to see what outdoor spectacles they have open for this year's summer season (there's usually a garden and a beach!).*

☐ *Check out what's on at this year's City of London Festival (colf.org).*

☐ *Go creepy-crawly hunting during National Insect Week (nationalinsectweek.co.uk).*

RUN FREE IN CORAM'S FIELDS*

Slap-bang in the middle of Bloomsbury, Coram's Fields is seven acres of kid-only fun.

Adults can't get into this secret green space without a child, which means that this is a centre-of-town-haven for little ones. There's a set of cracking playgrounds, with sand and low-rise slides for the tiniest nippers, right up to a high-rise wonderland with a zip-wire and huge, helter-skelter-style slide for bigger kids. It's bordered on all sides by low buildings and only has one entrance, so it feels extremely safe to let kids run free. We love to take a picnic (although no alcohol is allowed) and meet friends.

There's also a farm that houses goats, rabbits and chickens. It's very small, and a weeny bit sad, but kids will lap up the fluffy cuteness regardless. There are events all through the week including football sessions, soft play and art classes for small kids, right up to free after-school boxercise, music lessons and street-dance classes for teens.

The venue also hosts some fun annual events. We are regulars at the Guy Fawkes Night firework display, which starts earlier than most similar events and is geared towards tinier sparks-and-bangs fans, plus the Coram's gang hold plenty of seasonal fun days and holiday schemes.

Look for the tiny mice in the animal stalls, cheekily stealing the bigger creatures' food. Very cute!

---

coramsfields.org
93 Guilford Street, WC1N 1DN
020 7837 6138
FREE 🖥 ♿ 🛒
Open every day 9am–dusk
🚇 **Russell Square, King's Cross St Pancras, Holborn, Chancery Lane, Tottenham Court Road**
The ace Kipferl Café serves excellent Austrian coffees, as well as great vegetarian food. Plenty of high chairs.

SPOT BUTTERFLIES

It's high summer, peak time for butterfly spotting. Lazier than birdwatching, butterfly spotting can be done with an ice cream in one hand while sitting on a rug in the park. (Which sounds kind of blissful to us.) Butterfly Conservation run the Big Butterfly Count through the summer until the end of August, during which budding lepidopterists download identification charts and log their spottings.

All you need to do is sit in your garden, or head to a park, and note down every butterfly you spot over a 15-minute period. It's worth remembering that you can submit different spots on different days, so take your notebook with you if you go to a different park, playground or open space any time in July and August. Get out there, and get spotting.

Why not try Morden Hall Park (page 64) for excellent picnicking and butterfly-watching, Kew Gardens (kew.org), or the rare-plant-packed Chelsea Physic Garden, whose strange blooms attract all kinds of different insects.

bigbutterflycount.org
FREE July–August

Chelsea Physic Garden
66 Royal Hospital Road, Chelsea, SW3 4HS
chelseaphysicgarden.co.uk
££ 🍴 ♿ 🚼
Open summer season every day 11am–6pm, closed Saturdays
🚇 Sloane Square

The Garden of St John's Lodge
Inner Circle, near the junction with Chester Road, NW1 4NX
royalparks.org.uk/parks/the-regents-park/map-of-regents-park
££ ♿ 🚼
Open summer season 5am–dusk
🚇 Regent's Park, Camden Town

TOP TIP

Our secret butterfly-spotting garden is the Garden of St John's Lodge hidden in Regent's Park. It's half-hidden, and you might think it's private (the lodge itself belongs to the Sultan of Brunei), but push open the gate, wander inside and discover a beautifully kept series of circular gardens, complete with magical statues and hedges to hide behind.

IN A SECRET GARDEN

EXPLORE THE EIGHTH WONDER OF THE WORLD
AT THE BRUNEL MUSEUM

This tiny museum packs more of a punch than its size would suggest. It celebrates Isambard Kingdom Brunel and his father Marc, who were perhaps Britain's greatest engineers. They built the extraordinary Thames Tunnel, the eighth wonder of the world and the first tunnel built under a river, and on which the museum sits.

The museum tells the story of the beginnings of mass transport in Britain. However, it's the enormous secret underground chamber directly beneath the engine house that is the main draw.

Three times a week, and on other special occasions, there are walks that end in a descent into the tunnel to view the huge Grand Entrance Hall (££, but free for under-16s).

There are stacks of family events happening at the museum every summer, many located in the wildly beautiful rooftop garden. We love Hahahopscotch (no relation!)'s Sunday afternoon garden games (£). And parents can enjoy a cocktail from the pop-up bar Midnight Apothecary while their kids charge about.

A great little museum that goes out of its way to be family friendly. A real find.

Railway Ave, Rotherhithe, SE16 4LF
brunel-museum.org.uk
020 7231 3840
£ Under-16s go FREE
Open every day 10am–5pm
Rotherhithe, Bermondsey, Canada Water
Buggies are best left outside; bring your lock!

WATCH A PIG RACE AT THE LAMBETH COUNTRY SHOW*

The Lambeth Country show in Brockwell Park makes us very, very happy. It's a peculiar event, that has been bringing all the traditions of a village fair to the city for around 40 years, and we adore its quirkiness. Yes, the music line-up is great (we camp out in front of the little folk stage), but what really makes it special are the more off-beat offerings. Sheep-shearing, falconry, jousting displays and racing pigs all jostle for your attention. In true country-show style, there are competitions such as jam and scarecrow making, and (our personal favourite) vegetable character creating (the potato-headed Patrick Moore and the Damian Hirst-style skull made from sweetcorn and peas being all-time highlights).

There's also a really good selection of workshops on offer in country pursuits that have taken off in the city, such as urban beekeeping. It's a real opportunity for city kids to get a taste (and smell) of life outside the capital and have fun at the same time.

Norwood Road, SE24 0PA
lambeth.gov.uk/Country-Show
020 7926 7085
FREE but donate to keep it that way 🍺 ♿ 🛒
Open one weekend in July 11am–7pm
🚇 **Brixton, Herne Hill**

BUILD SANDCASTLES
AT THE ROUNDHOUSE'S BEACH

One of the most spectacular venues in London (it was converted from a railway shed and re-opened as an arts hub in 2006). There are evening shows that kids will love, from spectacular circuses to in-the-round theatre events, but hidden away under the main auditorium there are also studios for community use. Here, 11–16-year-olds can take part in arts-based courses including music recording, creative media and performing arts lessons, all at incredibly reasonable prices. Keep an eye out for free events and workshops in the main venue too (we loved their free Dads and Lads singing workshop).

Every year from July to August during the summer holidays, we hang out at the venue's 'beach' – a man-made resort on the terrace fitted out with tons of sand, ping-pong tables and huge screens showing sporting events, as well as seaside-style arcades and candyfloss. Go in the daytime when things are calm and enjoy the surreal experience of teaching your toddlers to build sandcastles on a rooftop in Camden.

Chalk Farm Road, NW1 8EH
roundhouse.org.uk
020 7424 9991
FREE–£££ ⬛ ♿ 🛒
Open July– August, Tuesday–Sunday 12pm–11pm, Monday 5pm–11pm
⊖ **Chalk Farm, Camden Town**

GET ARTY IN THE SUNNY GARDENS AT DULWICH PICTURE GALLERY

Dulwich Picture Gallery's regular, drop-in Artplay workshops are a great way to spend Sunday afternoons (they're held on the first and last of every month). The projects range from bunting to block prints, and are well conceived and well resourced, with talented session leaders. We really love the summertime sessions, where kids can sit outside in the stunning gardens and make art as part of a group (£). Take a picnic and sit lazily watching your kids get creative. There are also some excellent after-school and holiday-time courses where kids can explore an art form in more depth.

The picture gallery is a relatively crowd-free, quiet place that's close to Dulwich Village's great shopping. Take time out to go rare-tree-spotting around the gallery's gardens. Afterwards, pop across to the brilliant Dulwich Park to hire a tricycle, row a boat on the lake or feed the ducks.

Gallery Road, SE21 7AD
dulwichpicturegallery.org.uk
020 8693 5254
££ Under-18s go FREE 🍽 ♿ 🛒
Open Tuesday–Friday 10am–5pm (last entry 4.30pm),
Saturday–Sunday 11am–5pm (last entry 4.30pm)
Craft workshops on the first and last Sundays of the month, 2pm–4pm
⊖ **North Dulwich, West Dulwich**

Archikids is a weekend-long festival brought to you by the people behind Junior Open House weekend – perfect for your plastic-building-brick obsessives.

Held in the heart of the city, there are dozens of workshops, classes and drop-in activities related to architecture and building across the square mile. Try your hand at building a gigantic cardboard city, or a fantastical chicken coop (complete with real hens), customise giant, city-dwelling creatures, or ride a scooter around some of London's most interesting buildings.

Take a trip up to roof terraces not usually accessible to sketch buildings, or down low to the old Roman amphitheatre to build a city of bridges. Best suited to 5–11-year-olds.

Main festival hub, 155 Bishopsgate, EC2M 3YX
open-city.org.uk/
0207 383 5722
FREE &♿🧑‍🦽
Held Saturday–Sunday, see website for details 10am–5pm (last entry 4:30pm)
🚇 Liverpool Street, St Paul's, Moorgate

TAKE A TRIP UP A SKYSCRAPER AT ARCHIKIDS

DECORATE YOUR PAVEMENT

Adding water to chalk makes washable pavement paint, which is a great way to temporarily decorate concreted front gardens, drives and pavements (best check with neighbours if you're daubing on their doorstep). We like making our own bespoke games of Snakes and Ladders, or Hopscotch (of course!). You could allocate one paving slab per family member and see who comes up with the most creative use of their small space. Or how about making your own big, wiggly snake to try and walk along?

You could also play chalk trails; send one person off down the street or park track, who marks the ground with arrows and signs. The others wait five minutes, then try to track their friend by following the trail.

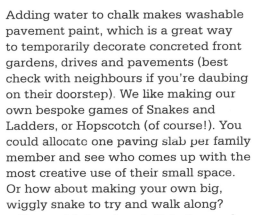

GET LOCKED UP IN THE TOWER OF LONDON

The power of the Tower isn't to be under-estimated. Packed with fantastically entertaining history, it's a full-on, blow-out, all-day experience.

Taking a Yeoman Warder (Beefeater) tour is essential. They know the place inside out and can deal with any amount of questions from inquisitive kids. There's also the spectacular displays of royal armour, the gruesome torture gallery and the Crown Jewels are an absolutely stunning example of vintage bling.

Check ahead to see what historical re-enactments will be taking place when you visit, and get there early to avoid the crowds.

It is pricy for families, but if you're really into palaces, it's worth getting a year's Historic Royal Palaces family membership, which will get you into five attractions across the city (**£££**). Tower Hamlets' residents can get into the tourist attraction for a measly £1.

There's also a very exciting way to get into the Tower for free (no, not blowing a raspberry at the Queen), which is obtaining a ticket for the Ceremony of the Keys. Those lucky enough to get (**FREE**) tickets for the daily event will witness the traditional locking up of the fortress – a ritual that has taken place for over 700 years. Visitors are admitted at 9.30pm for the ceremony, which takes about half an hour. Of course, it's a past-bedtime treat, and you don't get to see the Crown Jewels or any of the exhibitions, but for sheer atmosphere and excitement, it can't be beaten.

Tower Hill, EC3N 4AB
(hrp.org.uk/TowerOfLondon/WhatsOn/
theceremonyofthekeys)
0844 482 7777
£££ ⬛ ♿ 🚼
Open Tuesday–Saturday 9am–5.30pm, Sunday–Monday
10am–5.30pm (last entry 5pm)
⬤ Tower Hill, Fenchurch Street, London Bridge
Wheelchair and buggy access is limited in some of
the older buildings, but there are pushchair parks.

SCRAMBLE ABOUT IN LONDON'S BEST PLAYGROUNDS

Myatt's Fields

This recently restored park boasts a great playground with pirate ship, climbing wall and zip slide for older kids, but loads for little ones too. There are picnic tables in the playground and a shaded area with benches. Best of all are the fountains that come on between May and September, so cozzies and towels are a must, even when you're *sure* it's too cold for water games!

Our favourite part of the park is, however, the wildlife area where the kids can scramble about. The park's bandstand holds regular events year round (their free Christingle craft workshop and carol singing is particularly lovely).

Cormont Road, SE5 9RA
myattsfieldspark.info
FREE 🍵 ♿ 🚼
Open every day 7.30am–dusk
🚇 Oval, Denmark Hill
After your play, head to the Little Cat Café, which serves excellent coffee, locally made cakes, ice creams and has picnic tables at which to sit.

Diana Memorial

Probably London's best-loved and best-known outdoor kid-space. We just had to include it here because it's utterly brilliant. Inspired by Peter Pan, the centrepiece is a giant pirate ship, which in the height of summer is covered in tiny wannabe buccaneers, clambering around the treehouses, shuffling across walkways slung in the branches and sliding between encampments. The playground works really well for less able-bodied kids too. Only kids under 12 allowed.

If it's a hot day, finish up at the Diana Memorial Fountain. Teething problems with children, water and slippery granite have now been ironed out and kids adore dipping their toes in the cool water. Combine your visit with a trip to the **Serpentine Gallery** (their regular Sunday Family Days are lots of fun).

Bayswater Rd, W2 2UH
royalparks.org.uk/parks/kensington-gardens/facilities-in-kensington-gardens/diana-memorial-playground
0300 061 2001
FREE 🍵 ♿ 🚼
Open May–August 10am–7.45pm; April and September 10am–6.45pm; March and early October 10am–7.45pm; February and late October 10am–4.45pm; November–January 10am–3.45pm
🚇 Lancaster Gate, Queensway, Bayswater
If it's a nice day, go to the Boardwalk Café next door to sit outside and eat flatbread pizza.

Serpentine Gallery
Kensington Gardens, W2 3XA
serpentinegallery.org
020 7402 6075
FREE (suggested donation £) ♿ 🚼
Open Tuesday–Sunday 10am–6pm. Pavilion open every day 10am–6pm until the third week of October.
🚇 Lancaster Gate, Knightsbridge, South Kensington

Highbury Fields

Remarkably close to Highbury and Islington station, this play area, split into zones for different age groups, is spectacularly good. There's a climb-on train for tinies, a huge slide for slightly older kids and a gigantic spider's web of rope for bigger boys and girls to clamber around. Plus good clean toilets! There's also a little café with a great, fenced-in area with a few plastic ride-on toys where you can have a cup of coffee while your toddlers play safely.

Highbury Place, N5 1QP
islington.gov.uk/services/parks-environment/parks/your_parks/
greenspace_az/greenspace_h/Pages/highbury_fields.aspx
020 7527 2000
FREE ♨ ♿ ♘
Open permanently. There is a park keeper in the playground from 12pm until dusk every day.
⊖ Highbury and Islington

Queen's Park

There are two great playgrounds here for bigger and little kids, as well as a lovely sandpit. Cross your fingers for hot weather, so you can splash in the paddling pool (open 12pm–5pm). Older kids will love the petanque pitch (bring your own balls), and pitch and putt course. There's even a little pets corner (open from 11am) where you can pet pygmy goats and guinea pigs. Nearby parking isn't cheap, so try to come by public transport.

Kingswood Avenue, NW6 6SG
cityoflondon.gov.uk/things-to-do/green-spaces/queens-park/
Pages/default.aspx
020 8969 5661
FREE ♨ ♿ ♘
Open every day 7am–dusk
⊖ Brondesbury Park, Queen's Park, Kensal Rise

Brockwell Park

Brixton's favourite playground has undergone a relatively new revamp, and they've worked wonders with the space. The award-winning, elegant, wooden play equipment has loads of clambering space for older kids, with a cute sailing boat for the littlest ones. There's also a great sandpit and paddling pool, and a miniature train that runs on Sundays through the summer (page 105).

Norwood Road, SE24 9BJ
lambeth.gov.uk/Services/Environment/ParksGreenSpaces/
Parks/BrockwellPark.htm
020 7926 9000
FREE ♨ ♿ ♘
Open every day 7.30am–15 minutes before sunset
⊖ Brixton, Herne Hill

Don't forget!

Coram's Fields (page 118)

Crystal Palace Park (page 176)

Queen Elizabeth Olympic Park (page 58)

Regent's Park (page 140)

Bushy Park (page 85)

GO PLANE SPOTTING WITH A PICNIC

Very near to the Woolwich Ferry terminal and Woolwich Foot Tunnel is our secret plane-spotting place. The roar of the engines (bring ear defenders for small kids) and the rush as they pass overhead is a cheap thrill in itself, all plane geekery aside. Sit out with a picnic at one of our favourite plane-spotting sites:

Heathrow Airport

West Londoners have the third-busiest airport in the world on their doorstep (as they are constantly reminded by the planes overhead). Going inside the airport isn't really a fun experience (although the views from Terminal Five are stunning), so make your way to our pick of the viewing points, Myrtle Avenue, instead. Aircraft pass 12m above your head, shaking the ground as they go, and feel almost low enough to touch. Kids into planes will roll around on the floor in delight.

The viewing site is just around the corner from Hounslow Urban Farm (££) (hounslowurbanfarm.co.uk); combine the two experiences for a wildly varied day out.

Myrtle Avenue, Feltham, TW14 9QU
FREE
Hatton Cross, Heathrow Terminal 4

City Airport

Head through the University of East London's campus to reach the edge of Royal Albert's Dock. Grab a cheap cup of coffee on your way and you're all set to sit and watch the planes fly right over your head (they're a bit quieter here than at most airports due to noise restrictions). If you're feeling adventurous, the Capital Ring walk passes very nearby and you can follow its route through all kinds of strange and twisty Dickensian alleys.

Docklands Campus, 4–6 University Way, E16 2RD
FREE
Cyprus, Gallions Reach

Things to take

- ☐ Binoculars or a telescope
- ☐ A notebook to write down details of the aeroplanes you spot
- ☐ Something to sit or lie on to keep you warm and dry
- ☐ A camera to snap interesting flying machines
- ☐ A book to help you identify planes (try ABC Civil Aircraft Markings by Allan S Wright)
- ☐ A picnic!

COOK KEBABS WITH BABA GHANOUSH

Spice up an end-of-term barbecue with a Middle Eastern-inspired dish. Older kids will love helping to thread the kebabs onto sticks and toasting the pittas on the barbecue. Serves 4.

You'll need

For the kebabs
300ml natural yoghurt
a large handful of chopped mint
large clove of garlic, crushed
zest and juice of ½ lemon
salt and freshly ground black pepper
1 heaped tsp ground cumin
500g lean diced lamb
1 large red onion, cut into chunks
4 pitta breads
shredded lettuce, to serve

wooden skewers soaked in water
  for 20 mins

For the baba ghanoush
3 large aubergines
2 cloves of garlic,
  crushed with salt
juice of 1 lemon
½ tsp smoked paprika
2 tbsp tahini paste
drizzle of olive oil
freshly ground black pepper

1. Mix together the yoghurt, mint, garlic, lemon and salt and pepper and set half the mixture aside. Stir the cumin into the remaining half, add the lamb and turn the meat to coat in the marinade. Chill everything in the fridge for at least an hour.

2. Thread the marinated lamb and onion chunks onto 4 wooden skewers, and return to the fridge until needed. Remove the lamb and the reserved minty yoghurt from the fridge at least half an hour before cooking.

3. Light the barbecue, and when the coals are ready to cook over, prick the skins of the aubergines all over with a fork and place on the grill. Turn them with tongs and cook until the skin is charred all over and the flesh is soft.

4. Remove the aubergines from the grill and allow to cool slightly until easy to handle. Scrape out the flesh from the charred skins into a bowl, mashing as you go. Discard the skins. Mix the aubergine flesh with the rest of the baba ghanoush ingredients.

5. Meanwhile, grill the lamb kebabs for 3–4 minutes on each side, or until cooked through.

6. Place the pitta breads on the grill and toast on each side for about a minute. Turn with tongs to make sure they don't burn.

7. Slide the lamb and onion off the skewers and tuck them into the toasted pittas with a handful of shredded lettuce, a spoonful of baba ghanoush and a drizzle of the minty yoghurt.

TRAINS AND TUNES
AT ST PANCRAS INTERNATIONAL

Our very little toddlers love a day out at St Pancras Station, watching the trains (and people) arriving and departing. Have a look at the Meeting Point statue, the huge depiction of a kissing couple. Little kids love looking at the eye-bending frieze around the base; see if you can spot the lady with short shorts on, and rub her bum for luck (we're convinced it works).

The station even has a full programme of entertainment. The annual Station Sessions feature up-and-coming musicians (they gave a fresh-faced Ed Sheeran a break) and are a good way to introduce kids to live music. Keep an eye on the station's website for themed weekends and months – their Tiger Tracks events featured a free show from Brian May of Queen and storytelling by Bill Oddie, while Jamie Cullum once played an intimate free gig at the station.

There are also some great kid-friendly cafés on the stations's concourse (although you'll have to head next door to King's Cross to find our favourite people-watching branch of healthy, tasty, fast-food joint Leon).

Euston Road, N1C 4QP
stpancras.com
020 7843 7688
FREE �♿🛒

Open every day 7am–11pm
Station Sessions June–July, Thursday 5.30pm–6.30pm
Station Sessions Festival April–May/June
🚇 King's Cross St Pancras

THINGS TO DO

JULY

☐ Go avant-garde at the Sydenham Arts Festival (sydenhamartsfestival.co.uk).

☐ Freeze your own berry-packed, fruity ice-pops.

☐ Get community-minded (and have a lot of fun) at Lewisham's annual People's Day (lewisham.gov.uk/inmyarea/events/whats-on/peoples-day/Pages/default.aspx).

☐ Celebrate the last day of the school year with your own silly sports day (try a backwards running race and a slow-bicycle race).

☐ Head to beautiful National Trust property Osterley House for their annual, free, Osterley Weekend to try archery, dance workshops and their funfair rides (nationaltrust.org.uk/osterley-park/).

☐ Customise a T-shirt for summer.

☐ Hang with the hipsters at the Shoreditch Festival (shoreditchtrust.org.uk).

☐ Learn how to make a really good campfire.

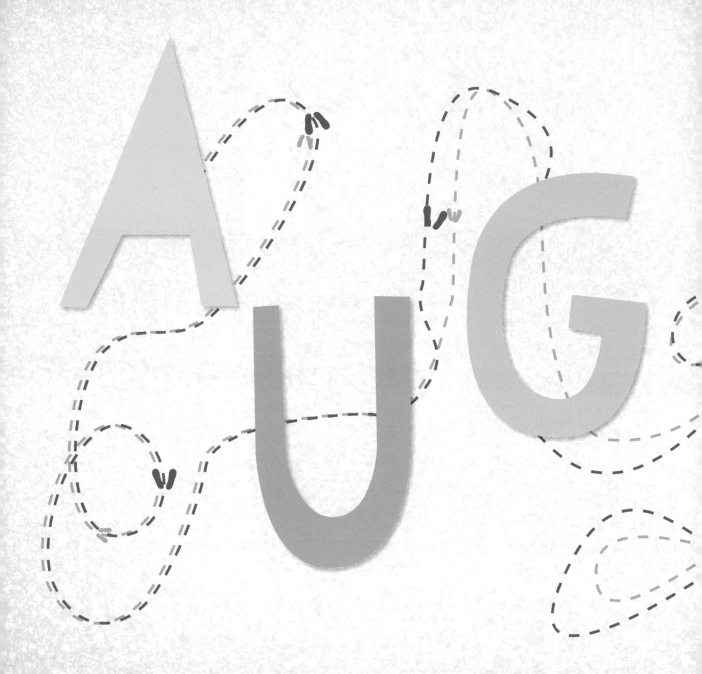

COOL OFF

August can be a hot and sticky time in London, so when the heat starts to feel oppressive it's time to dig out your swimsuits and towels and find somewhere to cool off. Here are our favourite places to get wet in the summer.

Jeppe Hein's fantastic aquatic sculpture Appearing Rooms has been on display at the Southbank Centre (page 36) every summer since 2007 and is an absolute must-do. Take towels and a spare change of clothes (or swimming costumes) and combine your free sploshing with an event at the venue. There's also a big festival involving lots of things to do and look at across the Centre each summer – there's usually a garden and beach involved.

Belvedere Road, SE1 8XX
southbankcentre.co.uk
020 7960 4200
FREE

Open every day 10am–11pm
Waterloo, Embankment, Charing Cross

The pool in the Victoria and Albert Museum's courtyard (the John Madejski Garden) is a great cooling-off spot if you're out on a trip to the big museums. The flat, shallow pool feels safe for kids, and it's big enough for lots of pairs of hot little feet.

Cromwell Road, SW7 2RL
vam.ac.uk
020 7942 2000
FREE

Open every day 10am–5.45pm, except Friday 10am–10pm
South Kensington, Knightsbridge

Surrounded by towers and concrete, the aptly-named Oasis Sports Centre is a council-run haven right next to Covent Garden. Beloved of nearby office workers, it gets really crowded at lunchtimes and early evenings in the summer, so try to go early or on a Sunday. Kids swim for £1 from Monday to Saturday.

32 Endell Street, Covent Garden, WC2H 9AG
better.org.uk/leisure/oasis-sports-centre
020 7831 1804
£

Open Monday–Friday 6.30am–10pm
Saturday–Sunday 9.30am–6pm
Covent Garden, Tottenham Court Road, Holborn

Brixton's huuuuge Brockwell Lido pool (50m long!) is a gorgeous, Art Deco wonder. It's been totally made-over, so the changing facilities are slick and the restaurant is absolutely lovely. Go on a sticky summer evening for fewer queues and lower prices.

Brockwell Park, Dulwich Road, SE24 0PA
fusion-lifestyle.com/centres/Brockwell_Lido
020 7274 3088
££ Under-5s go FREE

Open June–August, Monday–Friday 6.30am–8pm
Saturday–Sunday 8am–6pm
Herne Hill

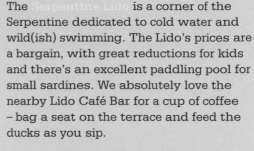

The Serpentine Lido is a corner of the Serpentine dedicated to cold water and wild(ish) swimming. The Lido's prices are a bargain, with great reductions for kids and there's an excellent paddling pool for small sardines. We absolutely love the nearby Lido Café Bar for a cup of coffee – bag a seat on the terrace and feed the ducks as you sip.

Hyde Park, W2 2UH
royalparks.org.uk/parks/hyde-park/sport-in-hyde-park/serpentine-lido
020 7706 3422

Open 10am–6pm weekends and Bank Holidays in May; 10am–6pm every day June–mid-September
Hyde Park Corner, Lancaster Gate

The elegant Edmond J Safra Fountain Court at Somerset House (page 98) springs to life when its water jets are switched on each morning. It's a great place to cool your heels and heads in the centre of London. If you're going to one of the venue's staggeringly good art workshops and it's a hot day, be sure to pack a change of clothes!

Strand, WC2R 1LA
somersethouse.org.uk
020 7845 4600
FREE

Open spring–autumn 7.30am–11pm
Temple, Covent Garden, Charing Cross, Embankment

BE FIRST TO HEAR THE NEXT HOT BANDS AT BRIXTON SPLASH

Always one of the most vibrant festivals in London, the Brixton Splash celebrates the many different and diverse cultures to which the area is home. Held on the first Sunday in August, there are stacks of performances from up-and-coming talents as well as a huge programme of music throughout the day playing on the four huge sound systems (take ear defenders for little ones).

The bill is spread across venues in the centre of Brixton, but if it all gets a bit hectic we recommend chilling out in the kids' arts and crafts area in St Matthew's Peace Garden.

Central Brixton, SW9
brixtonsplash.org
FREE
Open 12pm–7pm
Brixton

SEE A BIG SHOW FOR FREE DURING KIDS WEEK

Every year, the very top shows in London's 'glittering' theatreland offer children free tickets. West End's Kids Week actually runs from 1–31 August when limited numbers of young theatre-goers accompanied by paying adults get in for nothing. There are also 'activity packages' on offer that include backstage tours, workshops and Q&A sessions.

Pretty much every big show in London takes part, so, if you're thinking about going to see a show this year, August is definitely the time to do it. There are *enormous* bargains to be had, but you have to move quickly. Tickets go on sale in June; be sure to watch the website for the exact date to bag some.

Across London
kidsweek.co.uk
Ticketmaster 0844 847 1606
See website for events, dates and times

SAMPLE REAL FOOD AT BOROUGH AND MALTBY STREET MARKETS

Ah, Borough Market, foodie paradise and fun place to hang out for everyone. Get there early and let the kids see that not all food comes in colour-coded bags. If it's not busy, stallholders are usually more than happy to waggle octopus legs and make pigs' mouths 'talk'. Knock back a Monmouth coffee and let the kids choose a breakfast treat to eat in the grounds of Southwark Cathedral.

If we don't make it early enough to Borough Market to avoid the crowds, we prefer to have a wander through the food traders and pop-up grub stops on hipper-than-Borough Maltby St, with its converted railway arches full of delicious smells and appreciative 'Mmmmmmm' noises. Head to Monty's Deli for rolls loaded with salt beef and comforting chicken soup with matzo balls, or try to eat a whole stack of thick pancakes American-style in Bea's Diner.

Work it all off with a stroll down to the Golden Hinde – and then dash home before the crowds come out to play.

8 Southwark Street, SE1 1TL
boroughmarket.org.uk
020 7407 1002
FREE 🍽 ♿ 🚼
Open Wednesday–Thursday 10am–5pm, Friday 10pm–6pm,
Saturday 8am–5pm
🚇 London Bridge

GET A TASTE OF SOUTH ASIAN MUSIC AND FOOD AT MELA

Held on a Sunday in late August or early September, the gigantic festival of South Asian culture, the London Mela, has live music stages featuring Asian musicians, dancers and kids' activities, plus dancers, stalls and loads of Bollywood-style action. Musically, they turn up something different and vital every year; perhaps a London orchestra collaborating with the Bollywood Brass Band, or the first rumblings of something brand new on the Asian underground music scene.

The Mela also has a dedicated families' area, amazing food stalls and an eye-popping procession (our favourite ever starred a giant mechanical elephant, garuda bird and turtle).

Gunnersbury Park, W3
londonmela.org
FREE 🍽 ♿ 🛒
Open one Sunday late August/early September 1pm–9pm
🚇 **Acton Town, South Ealing, Gunnersbury Park**

RELAX, ROW A BOAT AND VISIT THE ANIMALS IN REGENT'S PARK

Sitting smack bang in the centre of London is the elegant Regent's Park. Head to this central green space for much more than the same old swings. There are pedalos and boats for hire; three playgrounds (four if you count Primrose Hill's fun park), three cafés (including our favourite, The Honest Sausage, serving free-range sausages and organic bread) and of course London Zoo (£££).

The zoo is a treat, but you can see some animals for free if you skirt around its perimeter, and sometimes they will let you in for free if you lurk around the gates about half an hour before closing time (shhh, we didn't tell you that!).

Chester Road, Inner Circle, NW1 4NR
royalparks.org.uk/parks/the-regents-park
0300 061 2300
FREE 🍽 ♿ 🛒
Open every day 5am–dusk
🚇 **Regent's Park, Baker Street, Camden Town**

ROLL ROUND BATTERSEA PARK WITH THE EASY SATURDAY SKATE

If you've spent all summer staring at those unworn skates, or putting off taking your offspring to the park to try out their new skateboards, don your elbow pads and helmets and get yourselves down to Battersea Park for a mass skate-a-long. The Easy Saturday Skate takes place at the Pagoda every dry Saturday at 10.30am and consists of two easy laps of the park (weather permitting). If it's your first time, relax – beginners are more than welcome and there are often qualified instructors on hand to help get you moving.

Battersea Park, SW11 4NJ
easysaturdayskate.com
FREE 🚲 ♿ 🚼
Open every Saturday (if dry) 10.30am
🚇 Battersea Park, Queenstown Road

CLIMB A SPIDER TOWER AT LEE VALLEY PARK

The Lee Valley Park is a 26-mile-long patch of greenery in the midst of the East London suburban sprawl. There are loads of facilities here, which is a legacy of the 2012 London Olympics – try white water rafting, kayaking, ice-skating and horse riding, among many others. The park is excellent for a cycle too; bring your own bikes or hire some.

The Park's farm has tons of fun things to see and do, even on a wet or cold day. Our kids are crazy for Rabbit World, and they have *the* most amazing play equipment, including a gigantic pillow to bounce on and a Spider Tower that parents will love as much as kids. If you've got pre-schoolers, go in term time and have the place to yourselves.

The huge park also has a campsite, which is a really great place to try out staying under canvas with a young family for the first time. Maybe you can sneak in a last-minute weekend away before the school term starts again. If there's a dire emergency, or if someone really doesn't like it or it's just too rainy, you'll be within striking distance of home. The site also has cute family cabins and cocoons for canvasphobes.

Lee Valley Park
visitleevalley.org.uk
08456 770 600
FREE ☕ ♿ 🍴

Lee Valley Farm
Stubbins Hall Lane, Waltham Abbey, Essex EN9 2EF
visitleevalley.org.uk/go/farms/
01992 892 781
££ ☕ ♿ 🍴
Open every day 10am–5pm
🚇 Cheshunt

HAVE A DANCE AT THE NOTTING HILL CARNIVAL

It's the highlight of the year for many Londoners (we know people who have made their home in the area largely so they'll have a great time at Carnival!). The biggest street celebration in Europe attracts over 2.5 million people every year. See the gentrified streets of Notting Hill burst into vibrant, colourful life, hear sound systems pumping out music from ancient ska tunes to ultra-modern hits-of-tomorrow and scoff some of the firiest, jerkiest food you'll ever taste.

It's a full-on festival of Caribbean culture that is wild and fun in your child-free days, but as with everything when you have kids, it's a different kind of fun with the nippers in tow.

Notting Hill, W11
thenottinghillcarnival.com
£ 🍽 ♿ 🚼
Open August Bank Holiday, Sunday and Monday 9am–7pm
🚇 Latimer Road, Notting Hill Gate, Royal Oak, Bayswater

HOW TO SURVIVE CARNIVAL

Here are our top tips for surviving the madness and having a harmonious, family day out:

- Use the home of any willing pals as a base.
- Make your travel plans well in advance; many underground stations are closed and buses diverted.
- Leave buggies at home. Use a sling or stick to piggybacks and shoulder carries.
- Track down Gaz's Rockin' Blues sound system. There's a real family feel to his patch.
- Remember your kids' ear defenders.

COOK JERK CHICKEN WITH RICE AND BEANS

If you really can't face the crowds, sit in your garden, fire up the barbecue, turn your stereo up and try this jerk chicken recipe that's (almost) as good as the stuff on the streets of Notting Hill.

You'll need

1 tbsp ground allspice
1 tbsp ground black pepper
½ tsp ground cinnamon
½ tsp ground nutmeg
1 tbsp fresh thyme leaves, chopped
4 spring onions, chopped
1 clove of garlic, chopped
3 medium fresh chillies, chopped
(reduce the amount and remove
the seeds if you don't want it too hot)
1 tbsp dark brown sugar
1 tsp salt
2 tbsp dark soy sauce
juice of 1 lime
6 chicken thighs and 6 drumsticks,
skin on

For the rice and beans
200g basmati rice
400g can coconut milk
a bunch of spring onions, chopped
2 large thyme sprigs
2 cloves of garlic, finely chopped
1 tsp ground allspice
salt
2 x 410g cans red kidney beans,
rinsed and drained

1. Place all the ingredients except the chicken in a food processor and blend to a paste.

2. Pour the marinade into a bowl, add the chicken and massage the marinade into the meat, making sure you get it underneath the skin. Cover and leave to marinate in the fridge for at least 6 hours, or overnight.

3. Preheat the oven to 180°C/350°F/Gas 4. Place the chicken on a baking tray in the top of the oven and cook for 25 minutes. Remove from the oven and use tongs to place the partly cooked chicken over a medium barbecue grill and cook for a further 5–10 minutes, turning regularly. Allow the skin to crisp and the chicken to take on the smokiness of the barbecue without burning. Brush the chicken while it is cooking with the juices from the baking tray.

4. While the chicken is cooking, prepare the rice and beans. Rinse and soak the rice in plenty of cold water, drain, then tip it into a large saucepan with all the remaining ingredients except the kidney beans. Season with a little salt, add 300ml cold water and set over a high heat. Once the rice begins to bubble, turn it down to a low heat, cover tightly with a lid so that no steam escapes and cook for 10 minutes.

5. Add the kidney beans to the rice, then re-cover with the lid. Leave off the heat for 5 minutes until all the liquid is absorbed. Serve with the jerk chicken.

For a new perspective on London, encourage your kids to look up. Enliven your strolls through the city by looking for statues; perhaps you could go on a lion hunt? Of course

SEARCH FOR

you know there are four lions in Trafalgar Square, but keep searching; there are over 10,000 statues of the fierce beasts lurking in London's urban jungle, a really handy game to play if you're stuck in a traffic jam, especially if you're on the top deck of a bus. Check out the excellent book *London Pride: The 10,000 Lions of London* by Valerie Colin-Russ for inspiration.

If you're walking through Soho, look out for the Seven Noses stuck to the side of the surrounding buildings. Plaster casts of human noses were placed there as part of an installation by artist Rick Buckley in 1997, and it's said that great fortune will smile on those who find them all. Worth a shot, eh? The noses are supposedly situated on Meard Street, Bateman Street, D'Arblay Street, Great Windmill Street, Shaftesbury Avenue, Endell Street and Floral Street, but some are really, really

THE SEVEN NOSES OF SOHO

tricky to spot. There's also a bonus extra nose on Admiralty Arch. If you can't find them yourself, take a walking tour (££, under-14s go free), peterberthoud. co.uk) led by a qualified guide.

SPOT PEREGRINES ON THE ROOFTOP AT TATE MODERN

Our kids are huge fans of birds of prey, with their hooked beaks, mean claws and meat-eating ways. There has been a peregrine's nest at Tate Modern for at least four years, and the birds shock tourists as they fly at speeds of up to 200mph. The RSPB set up a viewing area in the summer, with experts on hand to point out the birds and answer questions, and telescopes to peer through. Volunteers are located by the Millennium Bridge on the south bank of the Thames, opposite the Tate Modern tower.

It's one thing seeing these birds at displays and zoos, but quite another for kids to witness them careering around their natural environment.

Bankside, SE1 9TG
rspb.org.uk/datewithnature/146957-peregrines-at-the-tate-modern
020 7808 1240
FREE
Sunday–Thursday 10am–6pm, Friday–Saturday 10am–10pm
Southwark, Blackfriars, St Paul's

TATE MODERN

MAKE A DEN IN AN URBAN WOODLAND*

Another great woods for den-building is **Queen's Wood**, inexplicably less popular than the adjacent Highgate Wood, it's easy to lose yourself in this ancient forest (but not so much that you'll *actually* get lost). Wander off the pathways and under oaks and hornbeams until you find the perfect bivvy-building spot. There's even a really lovely organic café for when your little explorers get peckish.

Muswell Hill Rd, N10 3JP
fqw.org.uk
FREE 🚼 ♿ 👣
🚇 Highgate

A trip to **Sydenham Hill Wood** (or the adjacent **Dulwich Wood**) is like a trip to the countryside. The area is a mix of old woodlands, fragments of Victorian garden, new trees and the odd sculpture. It's a great place for wild play; run along the old railway track bed, scramble through the undergrowth, discover the ruined 'ancient monastery' (actually a Victorian folly) and make dens and shelters in which to hide from bears (and eat snacks). The Horniman Museum (page 62) is right by the woods, so afterwards head there for a cup of tea and look at the over-stuffed walrus.

Crescent Wood Road, SE26
southwark.gov.uk/info/461/a_to_z_of_parks/670/sydenham_hill_wood
020 7525 2000
FREE ♿ 👣
🚇 Forest Hill, Sydenham Hill

Epping Forest is London's largest open space. This huge forest is a wonderful place to go at any time of year, especially to build dens. There's miles of dappled shade, you'll feel alone in no time at all and there are trees galore just aching to be climbed. Although it's a wild wood, Epping Forest is really accessible for wheelchair users, with designated paths across the forest, and there are visitor toilets and cafés (we like the Larder at Butlers Retreat, near Chingford overground). If you're feeling particularly outdoorsy, there's a campsite (debdenhouse.com) that is great for a first night away under canvas, and allows campfires (woohoo!).

cityoflondon.gov.uk/things-to-do/green-spaces/epping-forest/Pages/default.aspx
020 8532 1010
FREE 🚼 ♿ 👣
🚇 Epping, Theydon Bois, Debden, Roydon

GET SPOOKED AT THE WELLCOME COLLECTION

The Wellcome Collection is a wonderful, weird place of ours. Their temporary exhibitions are always that little bit freakier and more fantastical than your standard museum, and err on the grisly. But what kid doesn't like bits of bodies, macabre medical tools and slightly disturbing art? Past exhibitions have included a celebration of skulls, a display of edible insects and an exploration of the relationship between madness and art, all shown in super-contemporary, cutting-edge settings. Exhibits can be a bit full-on, so it's worth checking suitability online before you set out.

There's a really great and well thought through programme of events related to each show; we've enjoyed a truly spectacular Day of the Dead celebration and a dirt-themed day of crafts and activities, and had a phenomenally interesting and insightful chat with a funeral director.

All this and a super, very kid-friendly Peyton and Byrne café on hand to supply delicious cakes and great coffee. No wonder we adore spending time at this strange and lovely venue.

183 Euston Road, NW1 2BE
wellcomecollection.org
020 7611 2222
FREE 🖥 ♿ 🛒

Open Tuesday–Friday 10am–6pm, Thursday 10am–10pm and Sunday 11am–6pm
🚇 **Euston, Euston Square, Warren Street, King's Cross**
The Collection is building a brand-new workshop space for teenagers, due to open in summer 2014, making the venue a real hub for 14–19-year-olds with an interest in science, art history and culture.

THINGS TO DO

AUGUST

☐ Enter the ballot for popular tickets for Open House weekend (page 157).

☐ Go bat watching on European Bat Night (we spot them in our back garden!).

☐ Freeze liquid watercolours in ice-cube trays overnight to make ice-paints.

☐ Catch a show in the cool environment of the Puppet Theatre Barge as it moves west for summer to Richmond (page 212).

☐ See your favourite TV stars in real life at London's biggest kid festival, Lollibop (**£££**).

☐ Watch the skies for shooting stars as the Perseid meteor storm reaches its height.

☐ Check to see what summer events the British Library (page 162) has planned – their workshops are ace.

☐ Take a trapeze lesson in Regent's Park with Gorilla Circus (gorillacircus.com).

☐ Create some crazy mocktails and set up your own pop-up juice bar.

SEPTE

TAKE A SURREAL CRUISE AT THE MAYOR'S THAMES FESTIVAL

This festival showcases London's aquatic artery using art, music and general weirdness, with cultural happenings taking place on, across and near the river. The celebration has expanded to ten days, and includes events such as huge waterborne operas, dramatic art installations, surreal river cruises, strange circus performers and pop-up fairs on bridges.

The legendarily spectacular night carnival and fireworks finale was cancelled due to lack of funds in 2013, but here's hoping that it re-appears in years to come – the atmospherically lit Thames water procession was one of our favourite nights of the year.

Westminster Bridge–Tower Bridge
thamesfestival.org
020 7928 8998
FREE–£££ &
See website for events, dates and times
Westminster, Embankment, London Bridge

BRUSH UP YOUR FOOTBALL SKILLS

Feeling inspired by the start of the football season? Hone your footwork at the Westway Sports Centre, a not-for-profit sports facility near Latimer Road. They run a series of drop-in, pay-and-play classes for different age groups from 5–15, which means you don't need to commit to a full term. If you've got two left feet (but strong arms), their excellent climbing wall may be more your thing.

1 Crowthorne Road, W10 6RP
westwaysportscentre.org.uk
020 8969 0992
£
Open Monday–Friday 7am–10pm, Saturday 7am–8pm, Sunday 8am–9pm.
See website for details of sessions
Latimer Road

TAKE TIME OUT
AT THE PHOENIX GARDEN'S AGRICULTURAL SHOW

If you've been running around the city and are hot, frayed and exhausted, make your way to this central green space, sit on a bench for ten minutes and recharge. Tucked at the back of St Giles Church, behind Charing Cross Road and Shaftesbury Avenue, it's a community garden run by volunteers who tend plants tailored to the tough, urban environment.

At midday you'll be rubbing shoulders with canny office workers with their lunches, so go early to have the place to yourselves (apart from some ladybirds, pigeons and the West End's only frog colony). The garden hosts regular events, the biggest being the first week of September's country fête, which the kids just love – we still can't quite believe that they manage to fit in sheep, cows and pigs, and still have room to spare for a brass band!

21 Stacey Street, WC2H 8DG
thephoenixgarden.org
020 7379 3187
FREE 🍽 ♿ 🛒

Open 8.30am–dusk. Fête, first Saturday in September, 12pm–6pm
🚇 **Tottenham Court Road, Leicester Square, Covent Garden**

KICK UP YOUR HEELS AT KLEZMER IN THE PARK

Every year, the usually staid Regent's Park bandstand on Holme Green, near the boating lake, rings with the sounds of Jewish party music at Klezmer in the Park. Klezmer is designed for kicking up your heels and letting rip, and our kids adore its frenzied rhythms and the extreme emotions it expresses. As well as the music, there's a kids klezmer dance parade, crafts, storytelling, a chance to explore Jewish history and even an opportunity to have a go at making your own music.

Inner Circle, NW1 4NR
jmi.org.uk
0300 061 2300
FREE ☕ ♿ 🚼
Open one Sunday in the first half of September, 1pm–6pm
🚇 Baker Street, Regent's Park

Set outside City Hall, on the banks of the Thames, The Scoop is a modern, sunken amphitheatre that springs to life during the summer months with free entertainment. Catch a play, watch a film or take part in a dance class or even an exercise session. We recommend checking out their London Free Festival, especially September's film programme, which shows a really good selection of kids' favourites, blockbusters and the odd classic. We also recommend taking cushions to sit on if you've got wriggly kids watching a long performance, as the concrete seats can be unforgiving on little bums. In our experience, it can also get really cold, even if it's a nice night, so take blankets and jumpers.

2a More London, Riverside, SE1 2DB
morelondon.com/scoop.html
020 7403 4866
FREE ☕ ♿ 🚼
Films start at 7.30pm
🚇 London Bridge, Tower Hill, Monument
Take the opportunity to visit City Hall (london.gov.uk/city-hall), home of the London Assembly. Parts of the building are open Monday–Thursday 8.30am–6pm, Friday 8.30am–5.30pm.)

SEE A FREE FILM IN THE OPEN AIR AT THE SCOOP

BATTERSEA DOGS HOME
REUNION DAY*

Woof! Battersea Dogs (& Cats) Home is the most famous animal shelter in London and each year it holds a reunion for all the hounds it's rehomed (there are usually around 1,000 in attendance). It's a day of cuteness and celebration, although be prepared to shed the odd tear when you hear some of the dogs' heartbreaking stories.

If it's a hot day, the dogs splash around in a paddling pool, and there are stalls and food for both humans and their four-legged friends. Dogs can take part in games including have-a-go agility races, and the genuinely side-splitting Temptation Alley, where they try to resist their favourite games and treats in order to win a prize, while humans can play on traditional coconut shies and bouncy castles.

We absolutely adore the dog shows, including the hilarious fancy dress category, climaxing in the Best Battersea Dog award. Be warned, if you haven't already got a pooch, your kids will be hounding you for one by the end of the day, and it'll be very difficult to resist.

Battersea Park, SW11 4NJ
battersea.org.uk/get_involved/events_challenges_battersea_
events_annual_reunion.html
FREE 🍺 ♿ 🍖
Open second Sunday in September, 11am–4.30pm
🚇 **Battersea Park, Queenstown Road**

SWING SWORDS AT THE WALLACE COLLECTION

It's back-to-school season. So if you're in the centre of London buying shoes and pencils, take time out to visit one of our favourite, tucked-away (and usually very quiet) museums, The Wallace Collection. Kids will enjoy the armour and sword rooms, with their racks of lethal-looking blades and shiny metal suits.

Where the museum truly excels for families, however, is its special events. The Collection's team arrange workshops, classes and talks around themes touched on in the museum's collections and, as there are a few different events to choose from, you can pick and choose the parts of the programme that suit the age of your kids. In the past, our lot have run around the exquisite galleries waving swords, made as much noise as is humanly possible at the museum's Loud Day, played marbles and created some really lovely bobbin lace at the 17th-century Day event.

Their two-day summer art classes (£££) sell out fast, and for good reason; they're brilliant.

Manchester Square, W1U 3BN
wallacecollection.org
0207 563 9500
FREE (£ donations suggested for special days) 🚇 ♿ 🚼
Open every day 10am–5pm
🚇 Bond St, Baker St, Oxford Circus

FIND HIDDEN WILDLIFE AT CAMLEY STREET NATURE RESERVE

Tucked in the concrete wastelands behind King's Cross, right next to the Eurostar Station of St Pancras, are two acres of wild nature reserve. Packed into this tiny pocket of greenery is a pond, a bit of woodland and meadow and a stretch of canal. We like the 'floating garden'; an ingeniously repurposed canal boat.

Older kids can volunteer at the park, and they also run events throughout the year; a spring festival, frog days, wassailing and pond-dipping.

Every September, the Reserve holds an Apple Festival. Join in apple-peeling games, try different varieties, make your own juice or even bake apples in a clay oven. Pip pip!

12 Camley Street, NW1 0PW
wildlondon.org.uk/reserves/camley-street-natural-park
020 7833 2311
FREE 🚇 ♿ 🚼
Open April–September 10am–5pm Mondays–Sundays; October–March 10am–4pm. Closed Saturdays
🚇 King's Cross St Pancras
Partial wheelchair and buggy access – some ponds and paths are inaccessible.

PEEP BEHIND LONDON'S LOCKED DOORS AT OPEN HOUSE WEEKEND

London's annual Open House weekend is an absolute highlight of our year. For one weekend in September, around 800 buildings across the capital that are usually closed to the public throw open their doors and let nosy Londoners take a peek. It's a great event regardless of your kids' ages – visiting houses works as well with babies in slings as it does older children more interested in architecture and secret spaces.

There are all kinds of buildings to snoop around. Past years have seen the BT Tower, Battersea Power Station, The Shard, the Gherkin and 10 Downing Street opened to all (although some of the more popular places have tickets allocated by ballot – be sure to register well in advance). However, it's often the smaller places that are more interesting. Private homes with stunning gardens or remarkable interiors, and breathtaking *Grand Designs*-style modern houses and teeny railway cottages are all open to anyone who knocks at their front doors.

Be sure to check out the programme of kids' activities too, for tours, architecture-themed workshops and concerts.

TOP TIP
Download the Open House app for up-to-the-minute news and easy-to-navigate guides to what's open.

openhouselondon.org.uk
FREE
Open one weekend in September 9.30am–5pm
Wheelchair and buggy access is dependent on where you choose to visit.

FLOAT DOWN THE THAMES
ON A RIVER BUS

Seeing London from the Thames is a totally new and fresh experience. We're so used to travelling over and under the river, it seems almost surreal to float down it, getting new perspectives on familiar buildings while enjoying a leisurely boat ride. There are, of course, privately organised tours and river-boat trips, but it's usually better value to take a TFL River Tour (£££). The tours run up and down the river, Westminster–Greenwich, Westminster–Hampton Court and Richmond–Hampton Court, as well as circular services (some trips are summer only). These tours include a commentary (sometimes hilarious, sometimes a bit odd) and are a great way to get from the centre of town to more far-flung attractions such as Hampton Court, the Cutty Sark (page 86) or the National Maritime Museum (page 52).

If you don't need a commentary, it's cheaper still to take the River Bus (££), which runs up and down the Thames all year. The River Roamer (£££) ticket is particularly good value, allowing you to hop on and hop off a boat all day – start early to get the most out of it.

tfl.gov.uk
020 7941 2400
££-£££ ♿ 🚼 **(some boats)** 🚆
Tours, around 10am to around 5pm,
for river buses, check TFL website
Use your Oyster card to get discounts on some services. A Travelcard on your Oyster will get you a third off some single tickets. Most boats have disabled access, but call ahead to check.

TAKE SOME FUNNY PICTURES AT THE GREAT GORILLA RUN

One of the funnest fun-races of the year, the Great Gorilla Run sees over 400 hairy-suited athletes pounding the pavements of London to raise awareness and funds for the Gorilla Organization. The route crosses Tower Bridge and takes in parts of the South Bank. It's a silly spectacle, so maybe kit out your kids with some old digital cameras (second-hand ones are as cheap as chips at jumble sales or on eBay) and see who can take the best picture. We recommend taking it in as part of a day out to the area; afterwards, you could take a stroll along to Borough Market (page 139).

greatgorillarun.org
020 7916 4974
FREE &♿ 🚶
Open third Saturday in September, 10.30am
🚇 **Tower Hill, Monument**

ENJOY EQUINE ACTION ON HORSEMAN'S SUNDAY

Having horse-mad kids in London is kind of tricky. There aren't an awful lot of ponies wandering our parks and gardens that they can pat, but there *is* guaranteed equine action every year at Horseman's Sunday, which takes place on the penultimate Sunday in September at St John's Church in Hyde Park. The event started in 1967, when the Hyde Park stables were under threat of closure, and now the blessing of the beasts is an annual event. Hot hoof it there for over 100 fancily dressed horses, a cloaked vicar astride a four-legged beast, bands, a fête and lots going on for children.

Hyde Park Crescent, W2 2QD
stjohns-hydepark.com
020 7262 1732
FREE 🚶♿ 🚶
Open penultimate Sunday in September, service at 10am, parade at 12pm
🚇 **Paddington, Marble Arch, Edgware Road**

MAKE YOUR OWN PINHOLE CAMERA

William Henry Fox Talbot (1800–1877) was the inventor of photography, and he worked on the technique at the Polytechnic on London's Regent Street (University of Westminster). For a bit of fun and education, make like the pioneer of snaps and build your own pinhole camera. This camera doesn't record pictures, but it does flip the world upside down when you look through it!

YOU'LL NEED

- A sunny day
- A stiff cardboard tube (maybe one that's had crisps in it and has a metal bottom...)
- Something to make a hole in the bottom of the container (a pin, very small screwdriver, thin nail or pen)

- Scissors
- Baking parchment or plain waxed paper
- A rubber band

1. On a bright and sunny day, get an adult to make a very small hole in the bottom of the container.

2. Cut the paper into a rough circle large enough to fit around the top of the tube with a 5cm margin (if you're using a crisp can, that will be around 17cm diameter).

3. Secure the paper across the top of the tube tight, like a drum, with the rubber band.

4. Go to a dark-ish room and point the hole side of the 'camera' at the bright sunny scene outside the window. The scene should appear upside down on the parchment. Try experimenting with using the camera outside too.

MEET ALICE
AT THE BRITISH LIBRARY

This is one library that doesn't tell you to shush. Their temporary exhibitions (££, under-18s free) are fascinating for older kids; we had a great time poring over the spectacular (and sometimes really funny) atlases and illustrations at their Magnificent Maps show. Their free, permanent exhibits are great too; our kids think it's cool to look at The Beatles' original, hand-written lyric sheets, are amazed at the Magna Carta and marvel at the exquisitely beautiful hand-written-and-illustrated, original manuscript for *Alice In Wonderland*.

There are some great, free, family-friendly workshops that generally take place during the summer holidays, and also children's literary festivals. We once spent a totally lovely afternoon listening lazily to stories in a colourful tent on the library's large courtyard.

The library has a great Peyton and Byrne café, perfect for munching on a few Mad Hatter's Tea Party-style cakes, or take your own lunch to eat in the piazza at the front of the building (which is also a great place for kids to blow off steam after they've been in the library).

96 Euston Rd, NW1 2DB
bl.uk
020 7412 7332
FREE–££ 🍴 ♿ 🚼
Open Monday–Friday 9.30am–6pm,
except Tuesday 9.30am–8pm;
Saturday 9.30am–5pm, Sunday 11am–5pm
🚇 **King's Cross St Pancras, Euston, Euston Square**

GO FOR A COCKNEY WALKABOUT AT THE PEARLY KINGS AND QUEENS HARVEST FESTIVAL

Events in London don't get much more traditional than the annual Pearly Kings and Queens Harvest Festival, which is held on the last Sunday in September. The unofficial royal family of the East End get decked out in their finest pearl-button-covered suits and spangly hats for a right knees-up, and no mistake, guvnor.

Starting at Guildhall Yard, there are donkeys and carts, Morris dancers, huge workhorses, mayors and 'traditional entertainment' (usually a Chas-and-Dave-style singalong), followed by a parade to St Mary-le-Bow church for a harvest festival service. We take our kids for their favourite treat afterwards – a pint of cockles (yes, really).

Guildhall Yard, Gresham Street, EC2V 5AE
pearlysociety.co.uk
FREE bring a food donation for the Whitechapel Mission & 🚼
Open last Sunday in September,
parade starts at 1pm, church service at 3pm
⊖ St Paul's, Mansion House, Bank

BANG A DRUM
AT RICH MIX

One of London's most exciting and inclusive arts venues, and right in the heart of London's hipsterland, Rich Mix is a non-profit-making place that truly reflects the ethnic diversity of the local community. There's a great cinema that shows blockbusters as well as arthouse films and one-off screenings. They have a brilliant Kids Club (£) at the weekend, as well as parent and babies screenings.

They also hold one-off festivals and events, often free, such as Chinese New Year celebrations, cultural festivals, storytelling events and a Jewish East End extravaganza.

On the third Sunday of the month we head to the venue's Mwalimu Express session. It's a perfect place to relax, soak up the sounds of African high-life music, take part in their toddler dance workshop, browse stalls, watch films and eat delicious African food.

The venue is also home to the monthly workshops of the pioneering world music and jazz group, the Grand Union Youth Orchestra. Every month they run jams for 12–25-year-old musicians, where they have a chance to play along with an artful blend of music from around the globe. If your kids like it enough, they might even end up with a place in the band!

35–47 Bethnal Green Road, E1 6LA
richmix.org.uk
020 7613 7498
FREE–££ 🎬 ♿ 🚼
Open third Friday–Sunday of January,
10am–5pm (last entry 4:30pm)
🚇 **Liverpool St, Old Street, Bethnal Green,**
Shoreditch High Street

THINGS TO DO

SEPTEMBER

☐ *Start thinking about which Christmas show you'd like to go to this year and book early to catch the cheap seats while they're still around.*

☐ *Watch a crazy variety of boats take part in the Great River Race, which pelts along the Thames from Greenwich to Ham.*

☐ *Find your nearest adventure playground and go for a supervised-but-thrill-filled play (londonplay.org.uk).*

☐ *Learn a new craft at one of the excellent, free, monthly Royal Academy art Sunday workshops (royalacademy.org.uk).*

☐ *Celebrate the Jewish festival of Rosh Hashanah by eating apples dipped in honey.*

☐ *Go on a hipster safari at London Fashion week; how many pictures can you take of crazily dressed fashion students?*

☐ *Catch some live music on Myatt's Field's Park bandstand in Lambeth (page 128).*

☐ *Melt down the stumps of old crayons in tubs to make new, multi-coloured ones.*

☐ *Look for the first conkers falling from the trees.*

☐ *Knit a scarf for winter.*

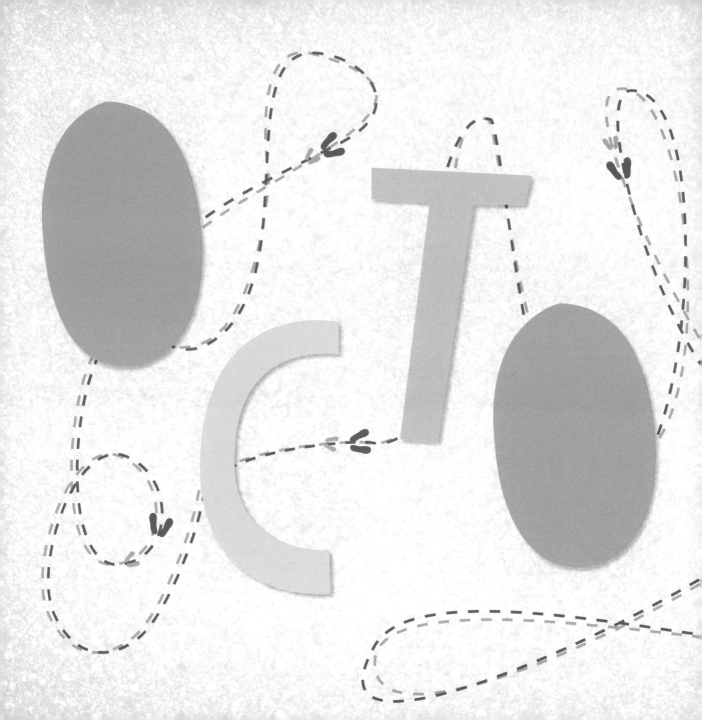

PLAY TRADITIONAL ASIAN WATER GAMES
AT THE JAPAN MATSURI

Hello Kitty. Manga. Massive swords. Martial arts. All things that kids love straight from the land of the rising sun. You won't want to miss this massive festival of all things Japanese that is held each October.

As well as food and drink to buy, video game characters to meet, clothes and gifts for sale, and music and martial arts displays, this is the perfect chance to try out some traditional Japanese activities for free. There's a taiko drumming area, calligraphy classes, chopstick games and kimono try-on stalls, and traditional Japanese games (usually water-based, so bring a change of clothes). There are also many modern Japanese cultural activities to pick from, such as the creation of a gigantic manga wall on which to show your prowess at cartoon art.

Fans of Japanese pop culture (or princess dresses) will love the hordes of gothic Lolita fans in their extraordinary Victorian-doll-meets-steampunk costumes, and top names from the world of J-Pop grace the event's main stage.

And don't miss the karaoke contest!

Trafalgar Square, WC2N 4JJ
japanmatsuri.com
FREE 🚲 ♿ 🚼
Open one Saturday in October, 10.30am–9pm
🚇 **Charing Cross, Leicester Square**

SEE GRUESOME EXHIBITS
AT THE HUNTERIAN MUSEUM*

The Hunterian Museum is home to pathological and anatomical curiosities, and is an ace place for kids. It's off the beaten track – to get to it you have to walk through the Royal College of Surgeons.

There are some truly disturbing and gruesome exhibits in this beautiful place; babies in jars, skeletons of giant men, deformed skulls, agonising-looking medical instruments and even Winston Churchill's false teeth, all of which will delight lovers of bizarre stuff.

For a gentle introduction, try one of the museum's special kid-friendly events, such as a hands-on workshop, meet-the-Georgian-surgeon Q&A or an object-handling session. Don't miss the excellent skeleton and internal organs coats (an excellent photo opportunity).

There's no café at the museum – if it's nice, eat your lunch in the green square opposite the Royal College of Surgeons.

The Royal College of Surgeons of England, 35–43 Lincoln's Inn Fields, WC2A 3PE
rcseng.ac.uk/museums/hunterian
020 7869 6560
FREE suggested donation £ 🖥 ♿ 🐾
Open Tuesday–Saturday 10am–5pm
🚇 **Holborn, Chancery Lane**
Wheelchair users and buggy pushers should use the entrance through the Nuffield College of Surgical Sciences next door.

GET SNAPPY AT WILDLIFE PHOTOGRAPHER OF THE YEAR

The annual Wildlife Photographer of the Year exhibition is displayed each October to March at the Natural History Museum. Packed with stunning creature-featuring images from all around the world, it's one of the world's most prestigious nature photography prizes. The show is hugely inspiring for aspiring snappers, as well as full of cuteness for animal lovers. You do have to pay to get into the exhibition, but you can browse pictures online.

Kids don't need to go to exotic locations to take pictures of wildlife, however. Try capturing a spider in his web in your kitchen or a pigeon on your windowsill. You can liven up a trip to the park or duck pond by holding a mini photography competition; digital camera technology means that you've got loads of chances to get a great shot, and most parents have a camera on their phone at least.

Remember, if any of your photographs are *really* good, you could enter them in the Young Wildlife Photographer of the Year competition.

Cromwell Rd, SW7 5BD
nhm.ac.uk
020 7942 5000
££ 🍴 ♿ 🚼
Open October–March 10am–5.50pm
⊖ South Kensington

TOP TIP
Check to see if the Horniman Museum is displaying previous years' winners work for free (page 62).

SPEND A CULTURED WEEKEND AT THE BLOOMSBURY FESTIVAL*

Each October Bloomsbury holds a weekend-long arts festival, with a *huge* number of events taking place. It's a festival designed with kids in mind, and many of the events are squarely targeted at families.

Bloomsbury has possibly the greatest concentration of interesting places in the world, from strange museums attached to UCL (the Petrie page 22 and the Grant page 92) to the Wellcome Institute (page 148). These places all host quirky events for the festival, such as Gumboot Dancing or creating a pop-up gallery (complete with a very odd taxidermied woolly monkey). Some houses, galleries and gardens that aren't usually open to the public hold tours too.

This area is also renowned for its literary past, which is reflected in the line-up of readings and events in many of the area's independent bookshops.

Look out for happenings at venues such as tip-top community garden-and-sports facility, the Calthorpe Project (their Apple Day usually coincides with the festival). The art installations in the trees in Russell Square are often extremely accessible for kids; in the past there have been swings strung up into trees, and giant white pods that open up to explore, and bounce in.

We never miss a walk down Store Street, a little road lined with independent traders, for their Shindig; it's a little festival-within-the-main-Bloomsbury-Festival. They've had painted pianos in the street for everyone to play, a slow bike race and a really funny try-on-a-wig stall. You could happily spend the whole weekend roaming the area and still not be able to take in everything that's going on. Bloom-ing brilliant.

//
bloomsburyfestival.org.uk
020 7713 0350
FREE ↓♿
Open Friday 6.30pm–8pm, Saturday 10am–10pm, Sunday 10am–10pm
⊖ Russell Square, Goodge Street, Euston Square
//

CONQUER THE CONKER CHAMPIONSHIPS

Polish up your nuts, and head to Parliament Hill for the yearly heritage festival and conker championships. There are traditional events (Morris dancing, welly wanging, a tug-of-war) taking place all day, but everyone is there for the conker contest, which takes place in the early afternoon. There may be a few bruised knuckles involved; some dastardly players soak their conkers in vinegar, bake them in the oven or even keep them for years in order to make them smash-proof. Not that we'd ever stoop so low.

There are categories for kids and adults, but if you don't want to take part, the spectating is excellent; it's great seeing the really serious competitors working themselves up into a frenzy.

Parliament Hill, NW5 1QR
cityoflondon.gov.uk/things-to-do/green-spaces/
hampstead-heath/Pages/default.aspx
020 7332 3322
FREE 🍺 ♿ 🛒
Open second Sunday in October 11am–4pm
🚇 **Kentish Town, Hampstead**

START SCRAWLING AT THE BIG DRAW

This month-long festival of illustration, design and scribbling will ensure your kids' 2B pencils are worn down to stubs. Heavy-hitting venues take part – events in the past have included a whole weekend of illustration fun across the V&A, where there were sessions in digital drawing on iPads, animal sketching, creating cartoon characters and shoe-designing classes. In the past, Big Draw participants have set world records, including the longest drawing (one kilometre) and for the greatest number of people to draw simultaneously (over 7,000!). It's exciting to be part of a world record; perhaps they'll try for a different one this year…

Big-name kids' book illustrators are like rock stars for tinies, and they often make appearances at Big Draw events; watch your nippers go wild for the likes of Quentin Blake and Axel Scheffler. It's a democratic, fun festival; all you need to take part is a pencil and some paper.

Across London
campaignfordrawing.org/bigdraw/
020 8351 1719
FREE
See website for events, dates and times

CURL UP
WITH A GOOD BOOK

Autumn is a time for staying in the warm with a good book, so get acquainted with your local library. As well as being the place to go to discover new stories, most also run free storytime and singing sessions for young kids, and some have toys to play with and space where you can read as a family. But if you're out and about in town, here are our favourite bookshops in London.

The Big Green Bookshop
This community-focused, fiercely independent shop is in the heart of Wood Green and is a beautifully curated gem of a place. There are three, free kids' morning storytelling sessions a week, as well as regular author events. The staff are incredibly friendly and knowledgeable; their recommendations are always spot-on.

Unit 1, Brampton Park Road, Wood Green, N22 6BG
biggreenbookshop.com
020 8881 6767
Open Monday–Saturday 9am–6pm, Wednesday 10.30am–6pm, Sunday 11am–5pm
⊖ **Wood Green. Turnpike Lane**

Foyles
The eccentric, huge flagship bookshop of this small chain is situated in the centre of town and is home to a massive kids' section. Their non-fiction and picture books sections are especially strong, and they hold great regular author events. But the best thing of all? Their tank of live piranha fish!

113–119 Charing Cross Road, WC2H 0EB
foyles.co.uk
020 7434 1574
☕ ♿ 🐟
Open Monday–Saturday 9.30am–9pm, Sunday 11.30am–6pm, (11.30am–12pm browsing only)
⊖ **Tottenham Court Road, Leicester Square**

Tales on Moon Lane

This magical bookstore is dedicated to children's and teens' books. As well as a squishy sofa and browsable shelves, it hosts storytelling events and visits from blockbuster children's authors. The staff are wonders at recommending new reads; we love their Book Basket selections for presents for newborns.

25 Half Moon Lane, SE24 9JU
talesonmoonlane.co.uk
020 7274 5759
Open Monday–Friday 9am–5.45pm, Saturday 9am–6pm, Sunday and Bank Holidays 10.30am–4.30pm
Herne Hill

The Golden Treasury

There's something pleasantly old-fashioned about London's largest independent children's bookshop. There are few bells and whistles (apart from in its small toy selection), but the stock choice is excellent, and its events are always packed out.

29 Replingham Road, SW18 5LT
thegoldentreasury.co.uk
020 8333 0167
Open Monday–Friday 9.30am–6pm, Saturday 9.30am–5.30pm, Sunday 10.30am–4.30pm
Southfields

Pickled Pepper Books

Although it's a relative newcomer, Pickled Pepper Books is already a fixture on the Crouch End family scene. It's a lovely place to hang out – kids are actively encouraged to stay and browse rather than being shooed out of the door. Its weekly storytelling events, music sessions and craft workshops are fun for smaller kids, while older children will love the serious and very grown-up business of the fortnightly teenage book group.

10 Middle Lane, N8 8PL
pickledpepperbooks.co.uk
020 3632 0823
Open Monday–Friday 9.30am–5.30pm, Saturday 10am–6pm, Sunday 12pm–4pm
Hornsey

Children's Bookshop

This granddaddy of kids' bookstores has been around since the early 70s. We have relied on the staff to give us recommendations for nieces, kids and friends for the last ten years, and they've never put a foot wrong. It attracts some of the biggest names in children's fiction including Andy Stanton and Axel Scheffler, while local resident Michael Rosen is practically the writer-in-residence. A marvellous place.

29 Fortis Green Road, Muswell Hill, N10 3HP
childrensbookshoplondon.com
020 8444 5500
Open Monday–Saturday 9.15am–5.45pm, Sunday 11am–4pm
East Finchley

SPOT DINOSAURS IN THE WILD

The life-sized sculptures of dinosaurs in Crystal Palace Park used to be one of our favourite parts of London when we were little, and now our kids love them just as much.

The 30 Victorian models may not be strictly accurate, but they are an exciting and unexpected find in the middle of a suburban London park. Some of them are on islands in the middle of a pond, while others swim in the lake. You won't be able to climb on the plaster models, as they're very old and fragile, but the great play area nearby has models you can straddle, and bones to swing from, as well as big dinosaur eggs to sit in.

While you're in the park, visit its amazing maze or the small children's farm (**FREE**) with its cute Shetland ponies. And there are also the remains of the Crystal Palace itself to search for (you can still spot the odd sphinx).

· ·

Thicket Road, SE20 8DT
bromley.gov.uk/info/200073/parks_and_open_spaces/780/about_crystal_palace_park
FREE 🍽 ♿ 🛒
Open Monday–Friday 7.30am–dusk, Saturday–Sunday 9.00am–dusk
🚇 **Crystal Palace, Penge West**
Download the free audio guide to the dinosaurs before you go, and learn all about their history, audiotrails.co.uk/dinosaurs.

· ·

SEEK OUT SPOOKY SIGHTS FOR HALLOWEEN

London loves to get spooky for Halloween and the celebrations at venues across the city seem to get bigger and scarier every year. Pretty much every museum and gallery will have something horror-filled going on, but we'll pick some favourites.

The **National Maritime Museum** is an atmospheric place at all times of the year, but when they wheel out the cobwebs and mist, it gets even more scary. They have an annual Halloween party (£) that lasts all day, often at the beautiful Queen's House. Be sure to dress up and try to win the fancy dress competition.

Romney Road, Greenwich, SE10 9NF
rmg.co.uk
020 8858 4422
Usually FREE Halloween party £ 🍴 ♿ 🚼
Open every day 10am–5pm (last admission 4.30pm)
🚇 **Cutty Sark, Greenwich**

London's **Canal Museum** is an unexpectedly appropriate place to celebrate Halloween. Its boat trips through Islington Tunnel are eerie enough as it is, but when ghosts and skeletons are added into the mix, they become truly scream-worthy. Boats depart all through the weekend closest to Halloween for a scary glide through the dark (or not-so dark earlier in the day). It's not dirt cheap (££), but all profits do go to charity.

New Wharf Road, N1 9RT
canalmuseum.org.uk
020 7713 0836
£ 🍴 ♿ 🚼
Open Tuesday–Sunday and Bank Holiday Mondays 10am–4.30pm, open on the first Thursday of each month 10am–7.30pm. Opening times around Halloween may vary.
🚇 **King's Cross St Pancras**

For two days only each year, the **Ragged School Museum** (page 44) turns into the Ragged Ghoul Museum! In the past they've had face-painting, activities inspired by Victorian ghostwriters (perhaps the spookiest of all the scribes), dressing up and mummy-making. And it's free!

46–50 Copperfield Road, E3 4RR
raggedschoolmuseum.org.uk
020 8980 6405
FREE (with a small donation) 🍴
Open Wednesday–Thursday 10am–5pm. Check website for Halloween opening times
🚇 **Mile End**
No wheelchair access beyond the ground floor.

MAKE

FIVE-MINUTE HALLOWEEN COSTUMES

Aaaaaargh! No, that isn't us screaming because we've seen a terrifying ghost, it's the sound we make when we realise that we only have ten minutes to get a Halloween costume together. Don't panic – here are our top ideas for quick-fix outfits.

• *Zombie princess (or zombie anything) – grab a party dress, or existing non-scary outfit, and paint your child's face green. A dribble of fake blood here and there and hey presto, zombie-princess, zombie-policeman, zombie-cowboy, zombie-whatever you've got lying around.*

• *Spooky tramp – rifle through Dad's wardrobe for an old hat and shirt. Tie a scarf to a stick. Hey presto, scary, Scooby Doo-style tramp!*

• *Superhero – chances are you've got at least one pair of superhero pyjamas around. Or a T-shirt. Make an eyemask, stick on the pyjamas and away you go. Or, stick a white shirt and a tie over the top of a Superman-logo T-shirt, stick on a pair of glasses and slick back your kid's hair – Clark Kent.*

• *A mummy – our top tip: don't use loo roll (the costume will disappear in less than ten minutes). Rip up an old sheet, making the longest strips of material you can, and use that.*

• *A stinging jellyfish – take an umbrella (preferably see-through) and tape streamers, ribbon, beads or strips of bubble wrap to it. Wear white clothes. For an added touch, take a pot of bubbles to blow from.*

COOK EYEBALL CAKE POPS

Why not host your own Halloween party and prepare a spooky feast? We make pumpkin pie, skull-shaped biscuits, 'brain soup' (rice pudding), 'dead man's fingers' (rolled-up bits of bread with almonds for nails and jam for blood) and jelly with spooky plastic figures suspended in it. These eyeball cake pops will look great at the centre of the table.

1. Break the fruit cake and biscuits/cookies into a food processor, pour in the melted milk chocolate and whizz to combine.

2. Tip the mixture into a bowl, then use your hands to roll into about 10 walnut-sized balls. Chill for about 2 hours in the fridge until they're really firm.

3. Push a lollipop stick into each ball and carefully roll the cake balls, one at a time, in the melted white chocolate to coat. Turn off the heat, but leave the bowl over the pan to keep the chocolate warm and runny. Use a teaspoon to pour the melted white chocolate over each ball to completely cover it. As you go, push the cake ball 'pops' into the foil-covered oasis or potato, then press a Smartie onto the ball's surface while still wet. Chill again in the fridge until the white chocolate has set.

4. Before serving, using the icing pens, add a 'pupil' to each Smartie and wiggly red veins to the eyeballs. Make your own variations; perhaps you could use white chocolate dyed orange to create pumpkin heads, or mini skulls.

You'll need

100g fruit cake
100g biscuits/cookies
100g bar milk chocolate, melted
  (in a heat proof bowl over a pan of
  simmering water; don't let the bottom
  of the bowl touch the water)
200g bar white chocolate,
  melted as above
a few Smarties and icing pens,
  to decorate

lollipop sticks
a block of oasis, used for flower
  arranging, or half a potato wrapped
  in foil

GET INVOLVED IN THE FAMILY FESTIVALS AT THE BARBICAN*

The Barbican Centre has to be near the top of our list of London places for families to visit. As well as its stunning exhibitions and inclusive art installations, the venue holds all-weekend, massive, themed family festivals (we've knitted, danced, sung, scratched our heads in puzzlement and laughed until we've had to visit one of the building's always-scrupulously-clean toilets). The children's library, with its regular kid-friendly events, is a great place to retreat to if it's all getting a bit hectic in the main building.

The backstage tours and promenade art performances that take place around the architecturally stunning-if-slightly-confusing spaces are ground-breaking and innovative, and the arts centre holds stacks of family-orientated orchestral concerts, ballets and operas. Plus the Museum of London (page 71) is just next door.

The Barbican is a wonderful place for Londoners. Even when there's nothing specific on, it's a great place to go and wander around.

Silk Street, EC2Y 8DS
barbican.org.uk
020 7638 8891
FREE–£££ 🍽 ♿ 🐕
Open Monday–Saturday 9am–11pm, Sunday and Bank Holidays 12pm–11pm
🚇 **Barbican, St Paul's, Moorgate**

NERD OUT AT THE LONDON SCIENCE FESTIVAL

The London Science Festival takes place yearly across the city at some of our favourite places; the Natural History Museum, the Royal Albert Hall, the Arts Catalyst and the London College of Fashion have all hosted events. Family events are held over the weekend of the festival.

In the past we've been to see 'Bridget', a Mars Rover and an exhibition of clothing that 'purifies' the air around us (we can think of a few kids whose emissions would benefit from a good pair of 'purifying' jeans). There are exhibits, workshops and talks too – most of the lectures are fairly highbrow, but not so academic that an older kid or teen interested in science wouldn't enjoy attending. A great introduction to 'serious' science.

Across London
londonsciencefestival.com/
FREE–£££
See website for events, dates and times

THINGS TO DO

OCTOBER

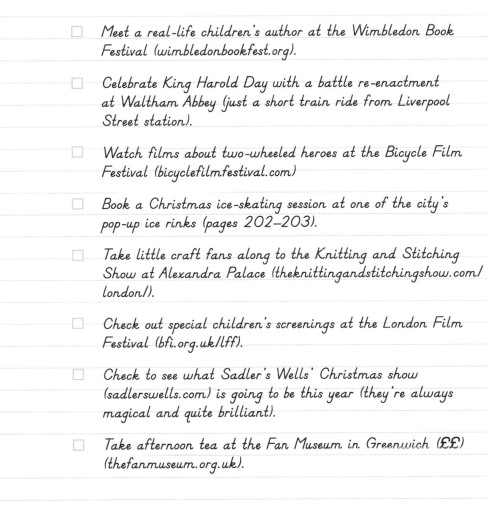

- [ ] Meet a real-life children's author at the Wimbledon Book Festival (wimbledonbookfest.org).

- [ ] Celebrate King Harold Day with a battle re-enactment at Waltham Abbey (just a short train ride from Liverpool Street station).

- [ ] Watch films about two-wheeled heroes at the Bicycle Film Festival (bicyclefilmfestival.com)

- [ ] Book a Christmas ice-skating session at one of the city's pop-up ice rinks (pages 202–203).

- [ ] Take little craft fans along to the Knitting and Stitching Show at Alexandra Palace (theknittingandstitchingshow.com/london/).

- [ ] Check out special children's screenings at the London Film Festival (bfi.org.uk/lff).

- [ ] Check to see what Sadler's Wells' Christmas show (sadlerswells.com) is going to be this year (they're always magical and quite brilliant).

- [ ] Take afternoon tea at the Fan Museum in Greenwich (££) (thefanmuseum.org.uk).

GET IMPROVISING AT THE LONDON JAZZ FESTIVAL

The London Jazz Festival gets into full swing for just over a week every November, but unless your kids are deeply into hard bop or funk fusion, they probably won't appreciate being strapped into a seat and subjected to full-on noodling sax solos. However, they *will* enjoy the festival's annual Jazz for Toddlers workshops. The workshops take place at venues across the capital, including Rich Mix (page 164), artsdepot (page 213) and Kings Place (kingsplace.co.uk), and start aspiring Jamie Cullums off on the art of improvisation.

Jazz sounds like a sophisticated concept for little musicians, but improvisation is what little kids do all the time; pretending a cushion is a hat, making up silly lyrics to songs they know well and inventing new dances. It's their stock in trade! There's music, storytelling and a chance to bash on some instruments. The classes always get booked up months in advance of the festival, so be sure to be as quick as you can off the mark when booking opens in September.

Across London
londonjazzfestival.org.uk
020 7324 1880
£

See website for events, dates and times

DANCE WITH SKELETONS ON THE DAY OF THE DEAD

The Mexican festival *'Dia de los Muertos'* (Day of the Dead) takes place on 1 and 2 November, and is fascinating for kids and adults alike. A colourful fusion of Catholic drama, traditional Mexican art and Aztec macabre tradition, it's the time of year to remember friends and family that have died. The festival's growing popularity sees London host more and more Dead-related events each year.

In recent years we've taken part in a Day of the Dead procession at the Wellcome Collection, gone deep into tunnels under Waterloo station for the Wahaca festival to make sugar skulls, cardboard coffins and look at Mexican art, and eaten a whole, delicious, hot heap of enchiladas, burritos and chimichangas. Look out for other celebrations of this colourful and crazy festival.

Across London
latinosinlondon.com
Day of the dead celebrations tend to vary wildly year to year, with few fixed events. Check listings nearer the time for details.

MAKE
SUGAR SKULLS

Mexican houses are decked out with these flower-sporting, decorated sweet treats every November. Make some to give to your friends. They'll keep for months or you can eat them straight away.

YOU'LL NEED

For the skulls

5 tsp meringue powder (try online)

1.125kg granulated sugar

skull moulds (we found some excellent silicone ones at wilko.com)

cardboard squares big enough to cover the bottoms of your skull moulds

To decorate

3 eggs

550g sifted icing sugar

2 tsp glycerine

food colourings

icing set

edible decorations (or inedible feathers, sequins and buttons if you don't want to eat the skulls)

1. First make your sugar paste. Add the meringue powder to the sugar and mix well. Sprinkle in some water, stirring and blending as you go until it forms a thick, sandy paste.

2. Push the mixture into the skull mould, making sure that it fills every nook and cranny. Put the cardboard square over the mould, and turn out the skull. If it doesn't come out, your mixture was probably too wet, in which case remix it with some more sugar. Leave your skull to dry overnight.

3. The next day, make the royal icing. Separate the eggs, and use the just the whites. Beat the egg whites in a bowl until they're foamy, then add most of the icing sugar. Keep beating until the mixture is thick. Add the rest of the icing sugar and the glycerine and beat again. Portion out the icing and add food colouring to each portion to create a palette of differently coloured icings.

4. Use your icing set with the royal icing and your decorations to create intricately patterned skulls. Get inspiration for decorations at mexicansugarskull.com

THE BEST FIREWORKS ON BONFIRE NIGHT*

November 5 is Guy Fawkes Night! At the top of our list is the child-friendly, free display at **Coram's Fields** (page 118). It starts earlier than most, at 5.30pm, has home-made cakes and soup on offer and is a gentler introduction to the joy of sparks. The fireworks are still loud and impressive enough to wow adults, but the display feels friendly and intimate.

Elsewhere, North Londoners should head to **Alexandra Palace** for a ticketed, all-day festival (££) with a funfair and cheap ice-skating sessions. The city provides a spectacular backdrop for the evening fireworks display. The event on **Blackheath Common** is huge, impressive and free, while Lambeth's fireworks rotate around the borough's parks – in recent years, they've been on at **Clapham Common**, **Brockwell Park** and **Streatham Common**.

Barnes Bonfire Night at the **Barnes Sports Club** usually kicks off with jazz from St Paul's School. Newham's free display (usually on **Wanstead Flats**) is accompanied by a laser show, and **Tower Hamlets** usually holds three simultaneous free displays across the borough.

Fireworks displays come and go, and times change year to year. Check the Hopscotch newsletter or London listings for exact details of shows before you head out.

If you can't face the crowds, head to your nearest high point (try **Forest Hill** or **Parliament Hill**) for a great view of all of London's fireworks. Your best bet is to go up at around 7pm.

Alexandra Palace
Alexandra Palace Way, N22 7AY
alexandrapalace.com
020 3390 0150
££ 🚻 ♿ 🚼
🚇 Wood Green

Blackheath Common
Shooters Hill Rd, SE3 0TY
lewisham.gov.uk
020 8314 7321
FREE 🚻 ♿ 🚼
🚇 Blackheath, Maze Hill, Deptford Bridge

Lambeth
Venue changes yearly
http://www.lambeth.gov.uk/Services/Environment/ParksGreenSpaces/EventsInParks/Fireworks.htm
0208 7926 6207
FREE 🚻 ♿ 🚼

Barnes
Barnes Sports Club, Lonsdale Road, SW13 9QL
barnessportsclub.org
0208 748 6220
££ 🚻 ♿ 🚼
🚇 Barnes

Newham
Wanstead Flats, Centre Road, E7 0DJ
newham.com
FREE 🚻 ♿ 🚼
🚇 Manor Park, Wanstead Park, Forest Gate

Tower Hamlets
Bartlett Park, Upper North Street, E14 6HS
towerhamlets.gov.uk
FREE 🚻 ♿ 🚼
🚇 Langdon Park, All Saints

Millwall Park
Manchester Road, E14 3AY
FREE 🚻 ♿ 🚼
🚇 Island Gardens, Mudchute

Weavers Fields
Viaduct Street, E2 6HD
FREE 🚻 ♿ 🚼
🚇 Bethnal Green

CELEBRATE THE END OF DIWALI

Diwali is the Hindu and Sikh Festival of Lights, which is celebrated across Asia and, of course, right across London too.

The biggest Hindu temple in London, the enormous and beautiful Shri Swaminarayan Mandir in Neasden, usually celebrates with a spectacular feast of fireworks, hymn chanting and a ceremony to bless accounts books. The temple is enormously welcoming at all times of the year, but especially at Diwali. Thousands upon thousands of visitors descend on the temple, which is spectacularly floodlit, bringing staggering quantities of edible offerings to add to the Annakut (or 'mountain of food') and ready to celebrate.

Outside of London's temples there are stacks more events to choose from. The biggest is in Trafalgar Square, which features live music and dancing (diwaliinlondon.com). Many of our favourite venues celebrate too; the V&A (page 192) has held a Diwali party in its own, deeply stylish way. The National Maritime Museum (page 52) also holds a festival that climaxes in a beautiful candlelit procession across Greenwich Park.

BAPS Shri Swaminarayan Mandir 105–119 Brentfield Road, Neasden, NW10 8LD
londonmandir.baps.org
FREE ☕ ♿ 🚼
Open every day 9am–6pm. Fireworks display in The Swaminarayan School Grounds at 8.30pm. Check website for closures due to religious observance.
🚇 **Stonebridge Park, Harlesden**
There is usually a special free Diwali Day shuttle bus service operating every ten minutes from Neasden Station to the temple from 3pm–11pm.

SEE GOG AND MAGOG
AT THE LORD MAYOR'S SHOW*

The Lord Mayor's Show might seem a quaint tradition; the great and 'good' of the city garlanding themselves in their finest jingle-jangle jewellery and parading through the streets on the second Saturday in November, but there's a lot more going on than stuffy old men in tricorn hats sitting in gold-encrusted carriages. The giant, wicker-woven figures of Gog and Magog, the guardians of the city, lend a pagan feel to the procession, while tanks, vintage cars, horses and marching bands create a show over which kids will go nuts.

The parade starts at Mansion House, via St Paul's to the Royal Courts of Justice in Aldwych. Then it returns by the Embankment. We like to watch the parade on the way out from Cheapside; it's near the start of the route, so the bands are fresher and more enthusiastic. Depending on how benevolent the Lord Mayor is feeling, sometimes there are fireworks in the evening.

Download the Show's app for up-to-the-minute news.

---

lordmayorsshow.org
FREE 🍺 ♿ 🚼
Open 11am–2.45pm
🚇 **St Paul's, Blackfriars, Mansion House**
Wheelchair and buggy accessible, but there are always big crowds, so check the website for useful access suggestions and viewing platform details. Use the Tube to get to the event; the buses will be in chaos with diversions.

GET CREATIVE AT THE VICTORIA AND ALBERT MUSEUM*

The V&A is not as immediately obvious a kid-pleaser as the Natural History and Science Museums down the road. Maybe this means that it just tries even harder, because their family-friendly events are superb.

Their themed days have a loose design connection but include a truly wide range of experiences. There are also regular art workshops where children might create jewellery, build a huge model city or design furniture.

Their Pop-Up Performances take place in some of the quieter galleries, and take inspiration from the exhibits. Ancient furniture might be highlighted with a puppet version of *Goldilocks*, or the Chinese galleries resound to the noise of dancing dragons. As Christmas approaches, look for wonderful seasonal performances; we caught a magical version of *The Nutcracker* performed Victorian-style one year.

Go on an out-of-season day with children to poke around the exhibits. Head up to the less crowded galleries to see original illustrations from Beatrix Potter, try out brass rubbing and explore the wonderful Theatre and Performance galleries with glittering stage costumes from musicals (and Kylie). There's even a dressing-up rail of spectacular clothes to try on and take pictures of. Don't miss the displays of toys and technology from the ancient days of the 1970s–1990s, as kids find looking at the things their parents played with endlessly hilarious.

Even if you bring a packed lunch, take a trip to the very special eaterie on the ground floor. It's the world's oldest museum café and is ornately tiled and totally beautiful; if you're really lucky, there may even be some live piano music to listen to. If you go in the summer, remember to take a towel and a change of trousers and go for a splash in the pool in the courtyard (page 136).

Cromwell Road, SW7 2RL
vam.ac.uk
020 7942 2000
FREE 🚆 ♿ 🍴
Open every day 10am–5.45pm, except Friday 10am–10pm
🚇 South Kensington, Knightsbridge
Eat your packed lunches in the Sackler Centre Lunchroom, or on the lawn if it's sunny.

ENTER THE ENCHANTED WORLD OF SYON PARK

West London's Syon Park throws open its gates on Friday, Saturday and Sunday evenings from late November to early December and becomes the Enchanted Woodland.

Once inside, you'll enter a magical world of twinkling lights, atmospherically lit trees and beautiful buildings (the Great Conservatory glowing from within is a gasp-inducing spectacle). Open from 5pm to suit little ones, it's a special treat to brighten a drab and drizzly winter day. It's a really wonderful way to kick off winter and make you feel all glowy and non-denominationally festive. Wrap up warmly and wear wellies.

Syon House, Syon Park, Brentford, TW8 8JF
syonpark.co.uk
020 8560 0882
££ 🖥 ♿ 🚼
**Open Fridays, Saturdays and Sundays 5pm–9pm
(last entry at 8pm). See website for opening
times throughout the summer**
🚇 **Syon Lane**

The Cinema Museum in Kennington is dedicated to keeping the spirit of classic film alive. Held in a tiny, 36-seater cinema complete with vintage seats and light-up signs, their charming Saturday Morning Pictures events take audiences back to the heyday of cinema, the 1950s, when kids piled into picture houses on Saturday mornings to revel in cowboy and Indian flicks, and cartoons. Expect all of that plus choc ices, cake and lots of engaging audience participation.

2 Dugard Way (off Renfrew Road), SE11 4TH
cinemamuseum.org.uk
020 7840 2200
£ ♿ 🚼
Open 10am, selected Saturdays
🚇 **Kennington, Elephant and Castle**

TRAVEL BACK IN TIME AT THE CINEMA MUSEUM

STEP INTO WARTIME BRITAIN AT THE IMPERIAL WAR MUSEUM

War! Huh! What is it good for? Absolutely nothing – unless, that is, its historical significance is put to good use in entertaining and educating your children, especially on a rainy day.

The Imperial War Museum is more a memorial and place for reflection than a celebration of battles, a fitting place to visit on Remembrance Sunday (the Sunday nearest to 11 November). Its line-up of kids' events is particularly strong, and includes crafts workshops (their make-do-and-mend quilt-making sessions were quite lovely), performances and storytelling. There are reconstructed submarines and wartime houses to walk through to get a feel for how soldiers and civilians lived during the wars.

Lambeth Road, SE1 6HZ
iwm.org.uk
020 7416 5000
FREE 💬 ♿ 🛒
Open every day 10am–6pm
🚇 **Lambeth North, Waterloo, Southwark**

PEEK INTO A MINIATURE WORLD AT THE DOLLSHOUSE FESTIVAL

Dollshouse collectors' obsessive miniaturisation is a world away from pink, plastic Barbie Glam Vacation Houses or Polly Pocket Spin 'n' Surprise Hotels. They collect, make and recreate gorgeous works of art, most of which are very unlikely to be played with.

November's Dollshouse Festival in Kensington brings together craftsmen who make the tiniest, most detailed furniture, collectors willing to spend top dollar on a perfectly crafted miniature bacon rasher and a huge selection of materials to make your own tiny dwellings. It's a lovely, traditional-feeling place to spend an afternoon, especially in the run-up to Christmas. Little doll-lovers will adore peeking into the tiny rooms and spotting the tiniest, most precise details.

There are workshops and activities for all ages in the afternoon, plus lots to buy, so strengthen your resolve before going through the doors.

Kensington Town Hall, Hornton Street, W8 7NX
dollshousefestival.com
020 7812 9892
£££ 🍽 ♿ 🚼
Open last Saturday in November, 11am–6pm
🚇 High Street Kensington, Notting Hill Gate
Cheaper family tickets are available from 2pm on the door.

WATCH OBSCURE KIDS' FILMS

AT THE FRAMED FILM FESTIVAL

Every November, the Barbican holds a children's film festival with screenings at the Barbican and other venues across London. Perfect for this dark, damp time of year, the series of film showings aims to bring international films to a younger generation.

There are also great workshops for young kids, some in association with big names in British cinema, such as BAFTA and Aardman. Past activities have included make-your-own animation days, human time-lapse animation workshops and make-up classes, plus chances to write film reviews. Older children and teenagers who are seriously considering a career in the movies are catered for with a series of seminars and panels aimed at aspiring directors, screenwriters and animators. There's even been the world's smallest solar-powered movie-theatre, the Sol Cinema, parked outside the venue, showing films created by young directors.

Barbican Cinema 1, Silk Street, EC2 Y 8DS
Barbican Cinemas 2 and 3, Beech Street, EC2Y 8AE
barbican.org.uk/education/series.asp?ID=1122
020 7638 8891
FREE–£££ 🖥 ♿ 🚼
See website for details
🚇 Barbican, St Paul's, Moorgate

MEET THE SNOW QUEEN AT THE SCANDINAVIAN CHRISTMAS MARKET

The Scandinavians do Christmas so well – creepy elves, ice-crusted fjords and the *real* Father Christmas. Every year, the Norwegian and Finnish churches in Rotherhithe host a Scandinavian Christmas Market.

We love making the journey down to Bermondsey for a browse around the atmospheric, tented stalls. The smell of spicy cinnamon buns hangs in the air, and there's a really appealing mix of hyper-tasteful Scandi-design Christmas decorations and rustic homewares, plus Moomin goodies, awesomely cute Fjällräven backpacks and obscure and authentic Scandinavian food. It's a really great place for original presents and festive things to eat.

Kids might even get to meet the Snow Queen, who, along with one of her elves, travels around the market on a giant snowball.

Albion Street, Rotherhithe, SE16 7JB
scanevents.co.uk/christmasmarket/
0870 933 0423
FREE 🍽 ♿ 🚼
Open last Friday–Sunday in November, Friday 10.30am–6pm,
Saturday 10am–6pm, Sunday 12pm–6pm
🚇 Bermondsey, Canada Water, Rotherhithe

THINGS TO DO

NOVEMBER

☐ Make a brightly coloured lantern for Bonfire Night.

☐ Meet some cute canines at the Discover Dogs Show (discoverdogs.org.uk).

☐ Get some ideas for your Christmas list at the tiny Pollock's Toy Museum (pollockstoymuseum.com).

☐ Book ahead for Christmas holiday art workshops — the Saatchi Gallery (saatchigallery.com) and Sir John Soane's Museum (soane.org) usually run some great ones.

☐ Make a pine cone hedgehog (just add googly eyes and scrunched-up sweet wrappers to make colourful quills).

☐ Buy a paper bag of roast chestnuts from the seller outside the British Museum.

☐ Browse back-issues of The Beano at The Cartoon Museum (cartoonmuseum.org).

☐ Make some gulab jamun (sticky sweets) for Diwali.

☐ Get into the festive season early and head to the South Bank for their German Market and carol singers.

GET YOUR SKATES ON AND HIT THE ICE*

A real London winter tradition, ice-skating is festive and something the whole family can genuinely enjoy. And it's the only time of year you get to say the word zamboni! ZAMBONI! Abandon your shopping, fretting, planning and panicking, take an afternoon out and strap on some blades.

Grand and traditional, **Somerset House** is the oldest of the pop-up skate places. It usually has a market, perfect for last-minute gifts. And don't forget its skate school, with classes that give confidence to even the smallest of sliders. The **Natural History Museum**'s ice is equally picturesque, and has the added appeal of nearby dinosaurs. Other rinks with traditional views and heritage include the two at **Hampton Court Palace** and the **Tower of London**.

The super-modern city building backdrop at **Canary Wharf**'s skate ring is dramatic, and has a great ice path that winds through fairy-lit trees. The London Eye's **EyeSkate** has spectacular views of the big wheel (and is close to the South Bank's festive markets). If you operate more on a last-minute basis, head to **Broadgate Ice**'s turn-up-and-skate, no-booking-policy rink. ZAMBONI!

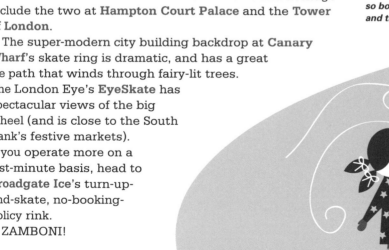

Somerset House
Strand, WC2R 1LA
somersethouse.org.uk/ice-rink
020 7845 4600
£££ 🍽 ♿ 🛒
Open every day 10am–10.15pm, selected dates 10am–11.30pm
🚇 Temple, Covent Garden, Charing Cross, Embankment
Sign up for their e-newsletter for priority booking and skate school info.

Natural History Museum
Cromwell Road, SW7 5BD
nhm.ac.uk/visit-us/whats-on/ice-rink
020 7942 5000
£££ 🍽 ♿ 🛒
Opening times vary through the season; check website for details.
🚇 South Kensington
Tickets for skating are on sale months in advance from their website's so book early for the best dates and times.

Hampton Court Palace
Surrey, KT8 9AU
hamptoncourticerink.com
020 8241 9818
£££ ♿ 🛼
🚇 Hampton Court
Open every day 10am–10pm
Tickets go on sale from late July.

Tower of London
Tower Hill, EC3N 4AB
toweroflondonicerink.com
020 8241 9818
Open every day 10am–10pm
£££ ♿ 🛼
🚇 Tower Hill, Fenchurch Street, London Bridge
*Tickets go on sale from late July. The season is shorter
than most rinks – November to early January –
so book early. The Thames Riverboat goes to nearby
Tower Pier for an atmospheric journey to and from the rink.*

Canada Square
Canary Wharf, E14 5AB
icerinkcanarywharf.co.uk
020 7536 8400
£££ ♿ 🛼
Opening times vary through the season; check website for
details.
🚇 Canary Wharf, Heron Quays
*The Canary Wharf shopping centre is great for Christmas
shopping, but you may need a city bonus for some shops ...*

London Eye
Riverside Building, County Hall, Westminster Bridge Road,
SE1 7PB
londoneye.com
0870 990 8883
£££ ♿ 🛼
Open every day 10am–9pm
🚇 Waterloo, Charing Cross, Embankment
*Tickets on sale from the summer; for a real treat, buy a
combination skate and London Eye ticket for a post-sunset slot,
and check out the Christmas lights from on high.*

Broadgate Circus
EC2M 2QS
broadgate.co.uk
££ ♿ 🛼
Open every day 9.30am–9pm
🚇 Liverpool Street
*Cheaper than most pop-up rinks, but take cash
– they don't take cards. There is also a car
park, which charges £7 for 2 hours.*

CELEBRATE HANUKKAH AT THE JEWISH CULTURAL CENTRE

Of course, lots of Londoners don't celebrate Christmas; the city's multi-culturalism is partly why we love it so much. However, things can be confusing for children whose classmates receive stacks of presents over the holidays. If you're of the faith, it's always worth checking to see what the Jewish Cultural Centre has on. Of course, there will be loads of Hanukkah-related shows and events, but we really loved the production of *The Latke Who Couldn't Stop Screaming* that the centre presented at the Roundhouse, which told the story of a fried potato pancake who gets confused by a village's Christmas preparations.

. . . .

Ivy House, 94–96 North End Road, NW11 7SX
ljcc.org.uk
020 8457 5000
FREE–£££ ♿
Open Monday–Friday 10am–9pm,
Saturday 9.30am–9pm, Sunday 12pm–6pm
◯ **Golders Green, Hampstead**

. . . .

BE INSPIRED TO START DANCING

Perhaps all those Christmassy shows have inspired your tiny dancers and they want to get serious about their moves. There are, of course, ballet classes and dance schools across the city, but we love the courses at Trinity Laban.

This dance and music school in South-East London is brilliantly inspiring; being around students and grown-up dancers brings an added gravitas to the kids' courses. Their Saturday morning Creative Dance classes take 2-and-a-half year-olds to 14 year-olds, and work on contemporary dance technique, but really emphasise creativity and expression. They are especially keen to recruit boys, and run many dude-only classes (with male teachers). Their Dance Ability classes are aimed at 5–12-year-old kids with disabilities, and are great for fitness and creative expression.

Laban Building, Creekside, SE8 3DZ
trinitylaban.ac.uk
020 8305 9400
FREE–£££ 🖥 ♿ ✗
🚇 Cutty Sark, Deptford, Greenwich
There are massive (two-year!) waiting lists for most dance classes at Trinity Laban. Book very, very early!

GO A TOUCH PAGAN AT WILD WINTER

It seems that the whole of December in London is swallowed up by Christmas, with no let-up until January. However, Greenwich Peninsula Ecology Park's Wild Winter Fayre – held on the first Sunday in December – puts a different twist on the festive season and celebrates more ancient traditions. Yes, there are gift and book stalls, but there's also willow wreath-making (the willow is cut from the park), wildlife trails and a chance to meet the Ice Queen, the North Wind and the Rainmaker. In Greenwich! Who knew?

Thames Path, John Harrison Way, SE10 0QZ
urbanecology.org.uk/
020 8293 1904
FREE ♿ ✗
Open Wednesday–Sunday 10am–5pm or dusk, whichever comes first; closed over Christmas and New Year
🚇 North Greenwich
The walk down the Thames path from the Tube is lovely. Be sure to borrow a pair of kids' binoculars from the bucket at the Ecology Park's gatehouse so that everyone can spot the wildlife.

LET THE GEFFRYE MUSEUM

INSPIRE YOUR DECORATIONS

One of our favourite, lower-key London haunts, The Geffrye Museum is dedicated to the history of the home. It does Christmas very well, and terribly stylishly too. You'll feel festive as soon as you step through the doors; all the museum's 16 display rooms are decorated in vintage style (from the spartan touches of the 1600s through heavy Victorian grandeur to kitschy disposable 60s plastic), and you'll all pick up some neat tips from their ghosts of decorators past.

The venue usually holds some excellent Christmas-themed crafts workshops through December, which have included holly-and-ivy decoration-making sessions and advent crown-making classes – the kids get creative and you get a free decoration for the tree – as well as traditional and modern carol-singing sessions. The Geffrye is not just for Christmas, however. It has great kids' activities through the year.

For a cheap, insanely tasty lunch, head to the nearby Vietnamese cafés at the bottom of Kingsland Road. We like the Song Que and the Viet Hoa.

136 Kingsland Road, Shoreditch, E2 8EA (between Pearson and Cremer Streets)
geffrye-museum.org.uk
020 7739 9893
FREE–£££ 🍴 ♿ 🚼
Open Tuesday–Sunday and Bank Holiday Mondays 10am–5pm
⊖ Old Street, Hoxton
The restored almshouse is not wheelchair and buggy accessible.

MEET FATHER CHRISTMAS

There are an overwhelming number of Father Christmasses to visit in London, prompting questions from our brood about which of these (obviously quite different) Santas is the *real* Father Christmas.

National Trust properties including Ham House and Sutton House often offer a gorgeously tasteful Christmas trail that leads to Santa's grotto and a present (£ plus entry fees). The Duke of York Square grotto is extremely classy (and FREE!), and there are complimentary treats such as hand and arm massages for mums and dads on certain dates.

The Museum of London's (page 71) Santa (£) sits in a traditional Victorian setting, and if you visit him, you'll have a chance to catch a Christmassy ballet or show at the Barbican. Across town, London Zoo's Father Christmas (a hefty ££ plus entry fee to the zoo) has, of course, got his own herd of reindeer, while the London Wetland Centre (page 26) Santa has real huskies and kids can have a ride in a dog-pulled sled! (£ on top of admission).

Our favourite Santa is at Kew Gardens; he's always sitting in a gloriously traditional grotto surrounded by Victorian carousels and fairground rides. Plus there's the always-dry, always-warm giant conservatory to wander around on even the coldest, wintriest day (£ plus entry fee £££).

Ham House and Sutton House (nationaltrust.org.uk)
Duke of York Square (dukeofyorksquare.com)
Museum of London (museumoflondon.org.uk)
London Zoo (zsl.org)
London Wetland Centre (wwt.org.uk)
Kew Gardens (kew.org)

TAKE A TOUR OF THE FESTIVE SIGHTS

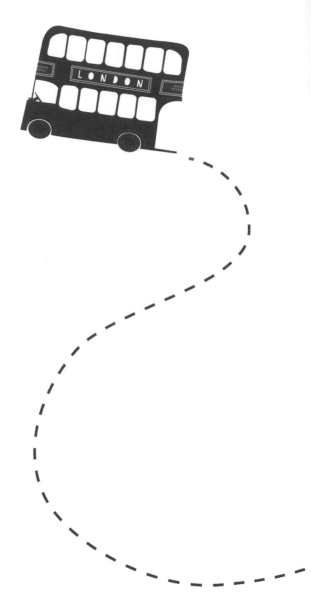

There's plenty about Christmas that's expensive and commercial, but there are simple pleasures to be had too. Sitting on a top deck of a bus, watching the twinkling lights come alive, or holding hands with Mum and Dad and looking into brightly lit shop windows on a winter wander.

Start in the early afternoon at the **Winter Wonderland** in Hyde Park. Even on the grimmest, rainiest day, it's an immersive, Christmassy experience. Their 45-minute Zippo Circus shows are great for really, really tiny kids (under-2s go free), and their Santa's Grotto is free too.

After you've visited the Wonderland, head towards Marble Arch and get the **number 6 bus**. Ride down the road to Selfridges. Hop off and have a good look at their glitteringly beautiful windows. Skip back on the bus, sit on the top deck and have a good look at the Oxford Street lights. Get off again at Oxford Circus.

Walk down Regent Street, taking in the lights, until you hit Great Marlborough Street on your left. Turn down the street and you'll spot the beautiful Liberty building. Liberty have our favourite Christmas windows; expect taxidermied animals or glimpses of a Victorian steam train, laden with toys. Take a stroll down Carnaby Street, which draws on its rock and pop music heritage for its Christmas look. It's pedestrianised, so a good place to watch buskers and street artists.

Duck into Kingly Court for brilliant independent shops (grab something for the littlest members of the family at Carry Me Home, carrymehome.co.uk). Kids will drool over the chocolate skulls, dogs and cakes

in Choccywoccydoodah and the cool cameras in the Lomo shop.

Head back to Regent Street, brave über toy emporium **Hamleys** if you can bear the crowds (it's the best place to get inspired for Christmas presents!) and climb back on the number 6 bus. Stay on the bus through the bright lights of Piccadilly Circus, and onwards to **Trafalgar Square**.

Make like you're in a Victorian fantasyland and grab a glimpse of the Trafalgar Square tree, which is lit in the first week of December and is still an essential part of the festive season in London. Schools and community group choirs tag-team beneath the sparkling spruce through the season, so you'll be hard pressed to miss out on hearing something festive. There's also a giant menorah in the Square, which is lit to mark Hanukkah.

Exhausted? Yes. Happy? Definitely.

Winter Wonderland
Hyde Park, W2 2UH
hydeparkwinterwonderland.com
020 8241 9818
FREE–£££ 💺 ♿ 🛒
Open November–January, every day 10am–10pm, except Christmas Day
🚇 Hyde Park Corner, Green Park, Marble Arch

Hamleys
188–196 Regent Street, W1B 5BT
hamleys.com
0871 704 1977
FREE–£££ 💺 ♿ 🛒
Open Monday–Friday 10am–9pm, Saturday 9.30am–9pm, Sunday 12pm–6pm
🚇 Oxford Circus, Piccadilly Circus

Buses
tfl.gov.uk/tfl/gettingaround/maps/buses
£ Kids go FREE ♿ 🛒 **(on most, but not all, buses)**

Trafalgar Square
WC1N 5DS
london.gov.uk/get-involved/events
020 7983 4750
FREE ♿ 🛒
🚇 Charing Cross, Embankment, Leicester Square
St Martin-in-the-Fields church on the square has an enchanting series of Christmas concerts every year and, of course, the very good Café in the Crypt. See stmartin-in-the-fields.org for details

LIGHTS, CAMERA, ACTION! AT THE CINEMA

If your lot find the Christmas crowds a bit of a struggle, give them a couple of hours respite and head to the cinema to catch a big festive blockbuster. Saturday morning screenings are great value. There are some truly excellent kids'clubs (best for over 5s, but some are for younger children) at various cinemas. Here are our favourite.

The Phoenix Kids Club

This wonderful independent cinema hosts a hugely popular Saturday morning club. Every week they'll show a recent film and a (bookable) activity beforehand for 20 lucky kids. The screenings are immensely good value, with the group ticket being a particular bargain. Kids over eight can attend unaccompanied. Mums and dads with really young children, check out the parent and child screenings and brilliant Toddler Time shows on Tuesday mornings.

52 High Road, East Finchley, N2 9PJ
phoenixcinema.co.uk
020 8444 6789
£ ⬛ ♿ 🚼
Open 11am, 12pm for screening
🚇 **East Finchley**

Picturehouse Kids' Club

Their Saturday morning kids' club shows recent blockbusters with a few classics thrown in. If you're likely to go more than once a year, the Kids' Club Annual membership will save you money. Kids over eight can attend without adults, so take advantage and drop them off while you go for a spin around the shops. Their regular baby-friendly screenings and Toddler Times are also great introductions to the world of cinema for teeny ones.

Across London
picturehouses.co.uk
0871 704 2068
£ ⬛ ♿ 🚼
Open Saturday mornings, times vary depending on cinema, more screenings during the holidays

The Lexi Kids' Club

Supporting your local independent cinema is a good thing. Especially if that cinema is a volunteer-run social enterprise. We're talking about *you*, the Lexi in Kensal Rise. Each Saturday, the Lexi wheels out a stash of craft bits and bobs and lays on a film-specific craft related to the screening. Mums and dads can relax with a cup of coffee or even a cheeky Bloody Mary.

194b Chamberlayne Road, Kensal Rise, NW10 3JU
thelexicinema.co.uk/special-events/kids-club
0871 704 2069
£ ⬛ ♿ 🚼
Open Saturday 10.30am
🚇 **Kensal Green**

SEARCH OUT GREENWICH'S ADVENT WINDOWS

Strolling around Greenwich in Advent is a wonderful day out; if you live more centrally, you can travel down the river to Greenwich by water bus (page 158).

Every day, a differently decorated window is 'opened' somewhere in the village (find a guide on their website); some are simple displays, others multimedia extravaganzas, and there's a lot of fun to be had looking for them. It takes a few hours to see all 24, so maybe plan ahead and just pick a couple of really good ones to look at (there are lots clustered around the main shopping and market area of the Village).

Of course, there may only be one or two windows open if you choose to visit early in December, so maybe combine your visit with a trip to the National Maritime Gallery, who often run Christmas-themed workshops.

adventwindows.com

FREE ♿ 🚢

A new window is unveiled every day between 1 and 24 December

🚌 Cutty Sark, Greenwich, Greenwich Pier (boat)

TAKE IN A FESTIVE SHOW AT THE THEATRE

Londoners are spoilt for choice when it comes to kid-orientated theatres, and most put on a big, family-friendly production at Christmas. We can guarantee that each of these theatres will have something seasonal, but not necessarily predictable, or over the holiday period. Here are some of our favourites.

Jacksons Lane

This arts centre in North London is right at the heart of the community. It hosts tons of productions and workshops aimed at children, often with a circus edge. At Christmas there is always a family show (past years have included really funny productions of *The Elves and The Shoemaker* and *The Enormous Turnip*), and on Christmas Day itself, the theatre throws open its doors for an all-day party for disabled and elderly people. The café in the foyer is a great meeting place for mums; plenty of space to park up the buggy and chat, and, in the mornings, it's often crowd-free.

269a Archway Road, N6 5AA
jacksonslane.org.uk
020 8341 4421
££–£££ 🍿 ♿ 🚼
See website for events and productions
🚇 **Highgate**

Puppet Theatre Barge

One of London's sweetest venues, this tiny theatre's performances are great for really little kids as well as older marionette fans. They make a special effort at Christmas, giving established shows a festive twist (*Brer Rabbit Goes to Africa* was changed to *Brer Rabbit Meets Santa* one festive season!). Seeing a show on the barge is a truly magical, immersive experience. And Little Venice looks glorious lit up at this time of year.

Blomfield Road (opposite No 35), W9 2PF
puppetbarge.com
020 7249 6876
£££
See website for events and productions
🚇 **Warwick Avenue**
During August and September the barge heads westwards to Richmond for its summer season.

artsdepot

A community arts centre, with shows aimed at all ages, but its kids offerings are particularly strong. As well as touring children's theatre companies, the centre has a programme of music and dance events that appeals to the whole family. Their stage shows are often aimed at very, very young children; they've put on *Catching Father Christmas*, which was great for 4–5 year-olds and *The Gruffalo*, which is a pre-school classic. Finchley toddlers love the free soft-play area, and it's a real hang-out zone for local families.

5 Nether Street, Tally Ho Corner, North Finchley, N12 0GA
artsdepot.co.uk
020 8369 5454
FREE–£££ 🍴 ♿ 🚼
See website for events and productions
🚇 **West Finchley, Finchley Central**

The Unicorn Theatre

The Unicorn has been producing and staging excellent theatre for young people and children since 1947, and sends its shows around the UK as well as hosting them in its bright, modern, huge building. Its Christmas shows tend to be inventive retellings of traditional, wintry fairytales that appeal to a slightly older audience than many of London's children's theatres. Even if you're not taking in a show, it's a good pit-stop; the café and baby facilities are excellent.

147 Tooley Street, SE1 2HZ
unicorntheatre.com
020 7645 0560
FREE–£££ 🍴 ♿ 🚼
See website for events and productions
🚇 **London Bridge**

Polka Theatre

Dedicated to shows for young people, Polka has two specially designed theatre spaces, a large main auditorium and an intimate 70-seater studio called The Adventure Theatre for very young audiences. As well as producing its own shows, the venue welcomes shows from around the world. Over past Christmasses, it's had a very sweet version of The *Wind In The Willows*, and a wonderfully icy version of Hans Christian Andersen's *The Snow Queen*. It's a lovely venue to hang out in, with a foyer full of toys and a Wendy house, and friendly staff. It also runs well-regarded workshops and courses for young drama fans.

240 The Broadway, Wimbledon SW19 1SB
polkatheatre.com
020 8543 4888
FREE–£££ 🍴 ♿ 🚼
See website for events and productions
🚇 **South Wimbledon, Wimbledon**

WATCH THE NEW YEAR'S
FIREWORKS

Older kids will go crazy over a trip to the New Year's Eve firework celebrations on the Thames, and it is a truly spark-tacular display. It's worth bearing in mind that viewing areas get full early (if you're not there by 9.30pm, forget it); there are long waits, long toilet queues and big, noisy crowds. However, those 20 minutes of super-sensational rockets and grand, sparkling set-pieces may well make it worth the effort.

If you can't face the jostling crowds, why not watch the fireworks from afar? Some of the smaller bridges, such as Lambeth, are much quieter. Alternatively, Primrose Hill, Alexandra Palace Park or Parliament Hill are great high points from which to see the display, or head for little-known vantage points around South East London. Steep streets in Forest Hill, at the back of the Horniman Museum on London Road, offer near-panoramic vistas of the London skyline and no parking restrictions. Happy New Year, everyone!

london.gov.uk/get-involved/events
FREE
Arrive by 9.30pm, fireworks start at 11.45pm
Embankment, Charing Cross, Waterloo

DECEMBER

- [ ] Go wreath-spotting; how many can you see on a trip down the street? Are they traditional or modern?

- [ ] Make a Christmas decoration or listen to a Christmassy story at the National Portrait Gallery, then go and gasp at the tree in nearby Trafalgar Square.

- [ ] Find 'Iron Lily', an ornate streetlamp originally powered by methane from the sewers, and now by gas, on Carting Lane, by the stage door of the Savoy Theatre.

- [ ] Find out about Christmas traditions in other parts of the world (and maybe steal some of the nicer ones).

- [ ] Go to St Paul's for their atmospheric carol service.

- [ ] Christmas is a time to think of others, so visit Postman's Park in EC1, a little square that commemorates heroic Londoners who died saving lives.

- [ ] Hold a fund-raising event for Shelter (shelter.org.uk), who help families at risk of losing their homes.

- [ ] Think about resolutions for next year. How about deciding to do even more fun things in London? Turn back to the beginning of the book, and start all over again!

LIST OF ATTRACTIONS AND EVENTS BY LOCATION

INDEX

ACKNOWLEDGEMENTS

Huge thanks to all the Hopscotch readers for their great suggestions and support.

To Jason Underhill, Esther Coles and Tom Hodges, Rhona and Colin Hodges, Sarah Rodriguez, Flora Patten, Katie Sullivan, Fiona Mottershaw, Sarra Manning, Victoria Hogg, Andrea Croce, Geoff Stoddart and Guri Hummelsund.

Extra special thanks to Elen Jones and Ed Faulkner at Virgin Books, Juliet Pickering at Blake Friedmann, Nicole Thompson, Sophie Yamamoto, Sarah Howlett and Helena Caldon.

ABOUT THE AUTHORS

Sunshine Jackson is a BAFTA-nominated documentary editor and edit producer. Sunshine spent three years at home after the birth of her second child, during which she founded the Hopscotch newsletter. Sunshine lives in South London with her seven- and four-year-old daughters, Florence and Bibi, her husband Jason and their cat Rosie. They never tire of the often-overlooked Investigate Centre on the lower ground floor of the Natural History Museum, and adore the fig tree in the wildlife area of Myatts Field Park (they've named it Tatty Bongle!).

Kate Hodges has been editing, writing and researching the Hopscotch newsletter since 2012 and has over 20 years' experience in magazine journalism. Kate lives in North London with her partner Gareth and three-year-old twins, Arthur and Dusty. Their favourite thing to do in London is to build dens in Queen's Wood in Highgate and run around the massive hangar full of planes at the RAF Museum in Colindale.

10 9 8 7 6 5 4 3 2

Published in 2014 by Virgin Books, an imprint of
Ebury Publishing
A Random House Group Company

Copyright © Kate Hodges and Sunshine Jackson 2014
Illustrations © Nicole Thompson
Design by Maru Studio

The Random House Group Limited Reg. No. 954009

Addresses for companies within the Random House
Group can be found at www.randomhouse.co.uk

A CIP catalogue record for this book is available
from the British Library

Printed and bound in Italy by Printer Trento

ISBN 9780753555293

To buy books by your favourite authors and
register for offers visit
www.randomhouse.co.uk